Thrift Store Mafia

The Times and Crimes of a Donation Attendant

Written by Travis Geier

Illustrated by Caylee Wells

Disclaimer:

This is a work of fiction. Unless otherwise indicated, all the names, characters, businesses, places, events and incidents in this book are either the product of the author's imagination or used in a fictitious manner. Any resemblance to actual persons, living or dead, or actual events is purely coincidental.

ISBN[Print]: 978-1-7377050-2-4

ISBN[eBook]: 978-1-7377050-3-1

Cover Art and Illustrations By: Caylee Wells

Edited By: Ann Klefstad

Annklefstad.com

Author Photo By: Brandon Evans

Instagram: @Brandonevans.art

www.goodlandartworks.com

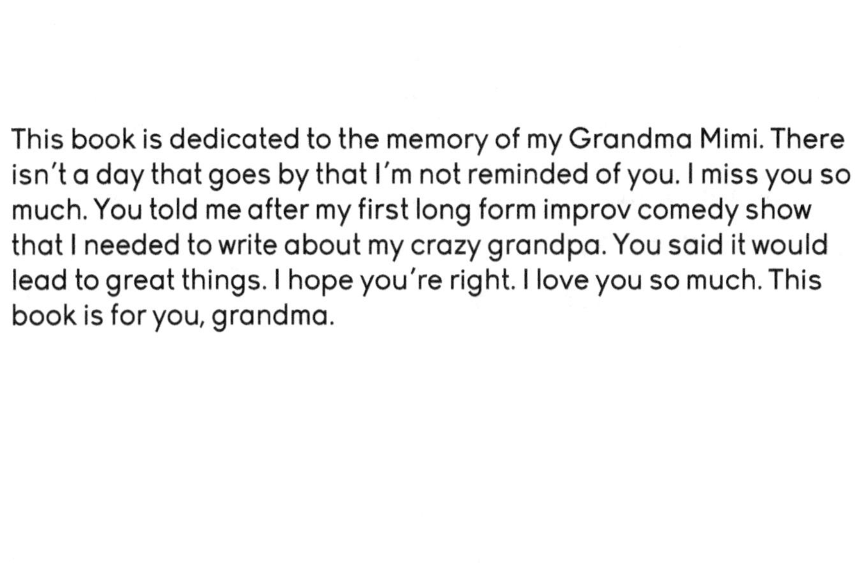

This book is dedicated to the memory of my Grandma Mimi. There isn't a day that goes by that I'm not reminded of you. I miss you so much. You told me after my first long form improv comedy show that I needed to write about my crazy grandpa. You said it would lead to great things. I hope you're right. I love you so much. This book is for you, grandma.

Table of Contents

Thrift Store Mafia

Prologue

After I moved out on my own, I lived in an apartment, a trailer park, and owned my first home. In all of these dwellings, a painting of a ship has been the focal point in all my living rooms.

It's an old ship in dark blue water with a dark green sky. The ship was painted with textured black lines squiggling around the ship, giving it an empty energy, a ghost presence. The textured part of this ghost ship painting is sprinkled with bits of gold. The specks of gold symbolize the pirates' treasure. I looked it up once and this painting is just a mass-produced painting you would find in a hotel in the 1980s. Where the painting is originally from has no meaning to me, but where the painting ended up is a trashy tale. The painting is near and dear to my heart because of its sinister significance.

The ship signifies a very strange, dark, and surreal time spent with my grandpa. Its banal pirate aura brings that time back to me.

The time itself is marked off from the rest of my life with the twisting lines and sprinkled gold of the ship. Grandpa and I worked at a thrift store together. He was the manager of donations and I was his donations attendant. In our eyes, I was my grandpa's first mate on a dastardly pirate ship, and he was the maniacal captain of said ghost pirate ship.

When we would come in to work at the thrift store, the aisles of furniture and knick-knacks would part into the giant tidal waves of our dark sea. We would hold on tight to get to the treasure. The treasure would pull up by way of a customer's vessel. We would unload our gold out of their automobiles in hopes of making it back to land with the treasure.

We would loot and pillage the bounty of the thrift store for our own need and greed. The customers whispered about us because they were scared. They feared us because of what we became. We would end up taking over the thrift store ship for our own. We became a Behemoth that destroyed the morals of the thrift store's mission.

As I sit here gazing at the painting of the ghost ship, it gives me two very different feelings. First, my body yearns for another adventure full of looting and pillaging with my grandfather. Together we would be the most wanted pirates of the lake country region! We were going to blast off the cannons to take on the world.

On the other hand, pirates must reflect on their wars that were waged with some form of regret. They hopefully dream of who they could have been if they were not criminals of the waters. I dream about what could have been if I was never a drug addict thief at a thrift store. I have children of my own now, and would never want my sons to live the pirate life that their father led.

In reality, I was young, bitter, and angry at the system. My pain had an effect on me. My grandpa was a crazy biker who loved to watch the world burn. We set our sails toward disaster. My grandpa fed into my mania as we steered our course towards what was sure to be wreckage.

On the other hand, my grandfather and I were about to set sail on an uncanny adventure. My grandfather and I had the map to the treasure and the keys to the store!

Oh, we were worse than Blackbeard, in ways that you could never imagine. We took something beautiful and turned it into tragedy. We failed to help others, but we helped ourselves, out of greed. We were the Thrift Store Mafia!

Smoking Weed with Grandma

Six months before my arrest, my life was spiraling out of control. It was 2006, and my first year out of high school. I thought it was temporary, that I was just in my party phase. I am crazy, so sometimes it's hard to catch myself before a big fall. I mean, "normal" gets pretty elastic. I wasn't seeing the behaviors that I was exhibiting that would eventually burn me. A weekend in the Twin Cities would foreshadow what was to come of the next few years of my life. It showcased the path that I was headed down…

I was a high school dropout. In high school, I had my mom meet with my guidance counselor to see what I wanted to do after high school. When we all sat down in the guidance counselor's office, she asked, "Travis, what do you plan on being after high school?"

I said, "I want to be a bum."

The counselor said, "How will you make money?"

"I will beg for it!"

My mom sat in the guidance counselor's office, red in the face with embarrassment. My guidance counselor just said, "Okay, then." We left that day with my future looking cloudy with a chance of complete failure in the forecast.

That next autumn, I had watched all my friends migrate to Milwaukee from our small city of Oconomowoc, Wisconsin. They were all attending colleges. I was stuck working at a Pick N Save grocery store as a bagger, smoking weed, and taking naps. I was going absolutely nowhere in life. I would cry to my mom because I was so jealous of my friends knowing exactly what they wanted to do with their lives. My mom would say, "You will find your purpose in life. Just because your friends are in college doesn't mean they know what they want to do with their lives. Even though it seems that way."

In the meantime, I was going nowhere fast. There was one friend of mine named Annie that was making similar choices. That is, she chose to not make a choice. Annie just decided to drive to Milwaukee every weekend to party. She was getting her college experience by going to keggers instead of attending classes.

Naturally, we hung out a lot because we both were burnouts going nowhere fast. We would smoke weed together. A lot. I sometimes would tag along to parties on the eastside of Milwaukee with her, but I did have a job, which made this form of education difficult.

Annie was planning a trip to Minneapolis to visit our friend Patrick who was enrolled at the University of Minnesota. I found out that my favorite porno grind band Anal Blast was playing their hometown of Saint Paul, Minnesota that particular weekend.

Anal Blast was a vile band whose songs were centered around women's menstrual cycles. Lead screamer Don Decker was this short, morbidly obese man who suffered from schizophrenia. I was called Crazy Travis all my life by my peers, so I was drawn to polarizing musicians like Don Decker or GG Allin. GG Allin was an underground punker that would poop on stage and throw his feces at his audience. GG Allin was infamously arrested in Milwaukee, Wisconsin while performing at the Odd Rock Cafe. GG Allin is dead, but I needed to witness the chaos that was Don Decker of Anal Blast.

I really wanted to make the trip, but I didn't particularly like our friend Patrick. He was an indie rock snob who looked down upon me since we were kids. Instead, I reached out to my friend Zed, who also was in his first semester at the University of Minnesota. Zed agreed to let me stay in his dorm, so I didn't have to stay with Patrick, the judgmental fuck.

Zed and I were friends later in our high school careers. He and I weren't super close in life; I mean, we hadn't been to each other's sixth birthday or anything. I told Zed that we would smoke our brains out before Anal Blast's set that night. In return, he was happy to offer me a place to stay. Back in high school, my other friend, Brian, and I were the first people to ever smoke weed with Zed. Brian and I were the first people to take Zed to the madness of a Gwar concert too. Zed was a good kid before Brian and I started to pollute his mind with THC and Gwar.

It was Saturday, September 30th, 2006 when Annie and I set out on our voyage towards the Twin Cities. The drive from Milwaukee is brutal, but we made fun out of it. Annie loved 90's club music, so we sang along with club hits like, "Rhythm Is a Dancer" and songs by Ace of Base. I really could be my goofy self around Annie. I showcased this when she would pop in a mix CD of Christina Aguilera.

We would dance in our car seats to "Genie In a Bottle" and we especially loved the song "What a Girl Wants." When "Genie In a Bottle" was blasting, I would put my hands together like Christina did in the video to show that I was a genie. We had an amazing time on the drive up there. That ended the second that Annie dropped me off.

Annie and I were occasionally having sex, so we didn't just act like friends anymore. She was making me keep the sex a secret from our friend group, but Annie acted more like a girlfriend to me; which made it very obvious to everyone.

Annie met up with Patrick, who acted like I was below him on life's totem pole, the turtle to his raven. Annie, Patrick, Zed, and I went out to a hipster pizza place that sells pizza by the slice. They had crazy pizzas like macaroni pizza slices. I got two buffalo chicken slices that night. The pizza was mediocre to be honest and being around Patrick was just dreadful. We all finished our pizzas, and Annie and Patrick soon split from the scene, leaving me alone with

Zed. When Annie dropped me off with Zed, she was very protective and cautious like a girlfriend because she knew that Zed was kind of a shithead. She said, "Be careful tonight because I don't want anything to happen to you."

We went to Zed's dorm. He said, "Bro! I joined a fraternity! We're going to party at their house on frat row!" I hated the idea of a fraternity, but I would tag along just to get through that Saturday night to see the almighty Anal Blast!

Zed stayed in the only University of Minnesota dorm in Saint Paul. That meant that we had to take a shuttle to get anywhere on campus because we were in the next town over. Zed was already pregaming hard with shots of liquor. Zed got so drunk that he made a huge scene on the shuttle ride to the frat house. You see, Zed was a big guy. He started to shake the bus back and forth while he screamed, belligerently drunk. Zed was acting very fake the entire time. To me, he was pretending to do all the tropes that you see of a college student. He was acting like the Big Man on Campus.

We got to frat row in Minneapolis to find that everyone in the fraternity was the douche-bag sports-guy type. They were nothing like me at all. None of them liked heavy metal. They all loved sports, drinking, and women. Zed was causing a big scene. He was pretending to be like every party animal from any teen comedy from the 1980's. Zed was just being loud, rude, and didn't seem to care about me.

I ended up just making small talk with some girls on the frat house patio. The girls said, "I'm sorry that you have to spend the weekend with Zed! You poor thing!" I agreed, while quite enjoying their sympathy. Zed was getting so belligerent that I ended up leaving the frat house without him. I thought it might be better to be away from the mess that Zed had become. I went to another frat house on frat row, and told Zed that I was headed there. Zed said,

"Okay bro, but the last shuttle back to my dorm leaves at 11:30, so give me a call."

Around 11:30, I dialed Zed. He answered, "Hello."

"How do I find my way to the shuttle?"

"Okay, bro! All you have to do is..." and silence.

"Hello, hello?" I looked at my cell phone, and the screen was black. THE PHONE WAS FUCKING DEAD!

I was now wandering around a huge city far away from where I needed to be. The city of Minneapolis slowly turned into a ghost town as I tried to figure out my next move. I figured that I may as well start walking to Saint Paul, but there was one big problem. It was 2006, so smartphones with GPS weren't invented yet. Even if I could make it back to Saint Paul by walking from Minneapolis, I still would never be able to locate Zed's dormitory.

I walked anyway. I started to walk in the direction that the shuttle had gone. I asked someone along the way. They gave me directions towards the city of Saint Paul. One guy said, "You're crazy! That is a hell of a long way, son!" I had no choice but to walk through the night.

I walked in a straight line from one big city to the other. The city of Minneapolis was desolate by this point. It was an urban desert. I came upon an old African American woman sitting in a walker at a bus stop. She took one look at me. She said, "You shouldn't be here! A white boy like you is going to get robbed in this part of town!"

I informed the old lady, "I have no choice because my friend left me stranded in Minneapolis. He lives in Saint Paul! I need to make it back to his dorm."

The old black woman looked at me from under her eyebrows and said, "Be *careful* then!"

Minneapolis is further north than where I live in Southeastern Wisconsin, and it was starting to get a lot colder as the night went on. It was colder than I was used to at night. Frost was starting to collect on everything. I was merely wearing a heavy metal t-shirt.

My skin and bones were starting to get cold which caused me to become exhausted. As I walked, I started to cry because I was desperate to find my way to the dorm. I made it to this park that had a cobblestone wall surrounding the back half of the park. I laid down behind it to block the gusts of wind. I tried to fall asleep, but the cold wouldn't let me achieve slumber. As I hugged my torso with my arms, I broke down in tears again. I was really homesick.

My tears turned to rage as I got up. I said, "Fuck this! I am finding warmth for the night!"

I became frantic and started to try the lobby doors of apartment buildings. The first lobby of an apartment was locked! In a rage, I tried another, but it too was locked! I walked at a fast pace to the next lobby, and the door opened!

I collapsed in the hallway where all the buttons are for tenants to buzz you in. I closed my eyes and fell into a deep sleep. It was very warm in the lobby which was comforting.

I awoke to someone shaking me. I looked up and saw a man and two women.

He said, "Rough night, huh?"

I got up and muttered, "Yeah, sorry."

I bounced out of the lobby back onto the streets of what was now Saint Paul. I had actually made it to Saint Paul, but I still didn't know my way to Zed's dorm. But it was daylight, at least.

I started walking in the direction that the shuttle had traveled in. After a while, I stumbled upon a marathon race. It was just like on television. The marathon was blocked off by police, there were a ton of spectators, and runners were whizzing by in hopes of a gold medal.

It was drizzling rain as I noticed a police officer in a poncho. He was wearing a black hat with a white and black checkered border that held his police badge. I walked up to the officer and said, "I'm from Wisconsin. I have been stranded all night in the Twin Cities. I need to get back to my friend's dorm in St. Paul. Do you know where to get on the shuttle that would take me to him?"

The police officer said, "Yes, but you need to get back to Minneapolis to meet up with the shuttle. The bus does pick-ups at the mess hall every half hour."

I was crushed that I now had to walk all the way back from St. Paul to Minneapolis, but I started to walk back.

I now had good directions to make my way to the shuttle. It was going to take most of the day to walk back from one big city to the other, but I would make it to the dorm.

It stopped drizzling and the sun came out as I walked to Minneapolis. It was garbage day, so all the city residents had their trash cans out. Suddenly, I spotted a little girl's bike sitting next to a trash can. It almost had a bright light of a halo above it like the bicycle was a gift from God. I was scared to walk up to the bicycle in fear the tires were flat.

The tires had air in them! I took off on the purple and pink girl's bicycle. The sun was shining and I was barreling through the city streets on a little girl's bike. I was jumping the driveways like I was a pro BMX rider. I was skidding as I came to intersections. I was having the time of my life now! I didn't want the bicycle ride to end.

I thought about just riding back to the dorm, but I still didn't know my way there. I needed the shuttle to drop me off. I sadly left the bicycle on a marble wall by the bus stop. I took one look back at her in sadness as I boarded the dormitory shuttle.

In about twenty minutes, I arrived back at Zed's dorm. It was the morning of Sunday, October 1st, 2006. Zed opened the door with a groggy look on his face. He hugged me and said, "Where have you been bro? I'm glad you're safe!" I told him the night's tale, and he laughed.

I said, "You need to find me some weed, dude. We need bud for Anal Blast tonight."

Zed said, "I will call around."

Zed proceeded to make phone calls to every dealer on campus, but it was dry in the Twin Cities. I was starting to get anxious because it didn't look like anybody had bud. He made one last phone call, and the guy said he had weed but it would be 20 extra dollars for a quarter.

I said, "I don't give a fuck. Let's go grab the bud."

We had to travel to the dorms in Minneapolis to meet the dealer, so we took another shuttle back. We met with this skinny Asian guy in a black beanie. He was very kind and seemed interested in me.

He said, "So you're from Wisconsin, huh? What's the bud like out there?"

"There's flame weed in Wisconsin, but you have to know where to look." *Flame* is what we used to call good weed. Now the kids call good weed "gas."

"I'm sorry that I have to tax you on the bud, but nobody has herb right now."

"I'm just glad you had some to sell me."

The Asian dude weighed out the quarter of weed (that didn't look that good to be honest), but it would do the trick. We departed the dorm, got on the shuttle, and headed back to Saint Paul. I purposely sectioned off some weed to save for when I got back to Wisconsin, and the rest we would blaze at the Anal Blast concert.

I gave Zed two giant nuggets. He then proceeded to roll the two biggest joints I had ever seen in my life. I tried not to be mad at Zed for the previous night's behavior. I was focused only on the Anal Blast concert later that night.

Later on, Zed and I headed down to Station 4 where Anal Blast was playing. Station 4 was primarily a heavy metal venue that hosted some of the genre's most extreme bands. Zed and I went inside to an almost empty venue. The only people inside were the band members hanging out by their merch stands.

A band with a bald singer got on stage and played a spine-splitting set! The band was grotesque death metal. After their set, I walked up to a bald-headed guy, telling him, "That was a great set, dude. It was absolutely brutal!"

He took one look at me and said, "You are a fucking poser! We haven't even gone on stage yet, douchebag." I was embarrassed, but in my defense everyone looked the same: bald heads, black t-shirts, and camo pants.

He grunted, "Go get me a beer you fucking poser boy!"

I was dressed in my Black Dahlia Murder t-shirt which made me look like an emo scenester. At that time, Black Dahlia Murder was considered a scene band, so I wasn't helping my case with the garments I was wearing proudly. I was flustered, so I walked off. Zed and I went outside.

Once outside, I noticed Don Decker of Anal Blast pacing around nervously outside. I walked up to him and said, "Don, I am a huge fan of Anal Blast. I traveled here from Wisconsin to see you guys!"

He took one look at me and literally screamed in my face, "FUCK YOU! YOU FUCKING EMO POSER! BURN IN HELL!"

That was strike two for me! I just watched and observed while Don paced around. He kept screaming, "I'm going to kill that motherfucker if he doesn't show up to play! The headliner Destroyer 666 came all the way from Australia to play with us. This motherfucker was smoking crack all night!"

Don kept having tantrums outside of Station 4. He eventually came up to me. He said in a soft voice, "I'm really sorry about what I said to you earlier. I'm just very stressed out because our drummer stayed up all night with a hooker smoking crack. We might not play now."

I sadly replied, "That sucks because I traveled so far to see you guys play. I discovered you guys on LimeWire and I've been a fan ever since."

"I hope we get to play because I have always wanted to play with the headliners, Destroyer 666."

I asked him, "Do you have that anime shirt with the little cartoon of a girl having her period blood spray out like a rainbow?"

"I'm sorry, we don't have any more of those t-shirts printed. What's on our merch table is it."

"I'm going to go check out what's available."

Zed and I went inside. I ended up buying the Vaginal Vempire shirt which consisted of a graphic of two lesbians engaging in oral sex. I put the shirt on and headed outside.

Suddenly, a red Ford Explorer pulled up. Some greasy guy with a beard got out. He started unloading a red drum kit. It was Anal Blast's drummer! I was so relieved that I would actually get to see Anal Blast play live! Don Decker seemed relieved as he helped haul in the drum set.

This was our cue to smoke the joints before Anal Blast's set. Zed and I went across the street to this brand-new playground that was surrounded by a black metal fence. The playground had that squishy rubber floor that is made of recycled sneakers and acts like a rubber cushion when kids trip on it. The playground was for an elementary school. Zed and I got on our knees, hiding from pedestrians.

I had Zed light these giant joints. We tried to power-smoke them, but it was quite the feat . . . I'm guessing that a 16th of an ounce was in each joint. We ended up getting so high that I almost fell over. I was the highest I had ever been as we smoked both joints to the butt. I was doubtful we could make it into the venue. Or find the venue.

About 30 minutes later, Anal Blast took the stage. They played a crushing set filled with little tunes about women's menstrual cycles. I left that night having a better night than the previous one. When they finished their set I felt a rush of relief that I survived the weekend lost in a strange city. I was on cloud nine to have this trip almost over!

Sadly, Zed died of an overdose in his early 30's. That moment on the playground is still a memory that I cherish. I can still close my eyes and see Zed holding those big honking joints in his hand. I almost wish that moment never ended, but it did.

I woke up on the morning of Monday, October 2nd, 2006 ready to go back home to Wisconsin. I met back up with Annie. I recounted my crazy weekend to her and Patrick. I said goodbye to Zed who had to go to class.

Annie and I drove 5 hours back to Wisconsin. We jammed out to Christina Aguilera and Ace of Base like always. Annie pulled into the gravel driveway of my parent's house. I noticed my grandma's white Rav 4 in my mom's driveway. I kissed Annie goodbye. I was eager to see what my grandma was doing here.

Unlike the weather in Minnesota, it was a hot day. The sky was turning pink, purple, and orange as it began to settle into nightfall. My grandma and mom were in comfy chairs on the deck of my mom's lake house. I remember my grandma wearing a navy blue baseball cap as she sat with my mother.

I came up and greeted them. In the last year or two, my grandma and grandpa had gotten a divorce. My grandparents were in a 12-step program for most of my life, but my mom recently told me that my grandma went to a bonfire in Fox Lake, Wisconsin. At the bonfire, my grandma got drunk and smoked marijuana. My grandma seemed different that night, like I might be able to get her to smoke weed with her 18-year-old grandson.

My grandma had a bad track record with polluting marijuana into her children's minds. In the 1970s, my grandma was a drinker and a stoner. On top of that, she had very unorthodox parenting practices. My aunt recalled my grandmother's smoking habits while she and my mom were little girls. The following is the story told by my aunt:

"There are two times that stand out in my mind in regards to smoking weed with my family. My sister and I were introduced to weed at the ages of 9 and 10. One evening in our living room, my then 16-year-old uncle Dori was rolling a joint. We asked, 'What's that?'

"He replied with 'I'm rolling a joint'. Of course, we asked if we could do it too. The three of us sat on the long green sofa, elbow to elbow, with our tiny rolling papers in our laps and rolled our joints, carefully licking the edge of the delicate paper to seal it. Uncle Dori said, 'Now we smoke them'

"Meanwhile, my mother and Aunt Nicki were in the kitchen, sipping Amaretto. I feel it's important to mention their ages also, if only to excuse my mother for her lack of parenting skills. My mother was 27 and Aunt Nicki must have been around 20. They came into the living room to get Dori as they were ready to go out. My mother noticed that my sister and I were stoned; she clearly was not happy about it. She asked Dori, sharply, 'Did you get the kids stoned?'

"I'm sure she continued to berate him in the car enroute to whatever bar they were heading to. Meanwhile at home, it was my sister's day to do the dishes, so she headed to the kitchen while I lay on the sofa zoning out. I remember after a while she came in to see what I was up to. She asked me 'what are you doing with your eyes?' I was staring at the ceiling, and it really freaked her out because she begged me to tell her that I was ok.

"Another episode was when my mom, Aunt Nicki, and I were sitting at the dining room table. It was not very long after the first incident, so I was probably still 9 or maybe 10 by this time.

My sister had gone to a friend's house. I always felt abandoned when she would choose to go be with her friends rather than stay with me. As I sat at the table with my mother and aunt, somehow the joint got passed to me. I suppose I must have asked for it, and maybe they were sensitive to my gloominess from being left behind, so they passed me the joint.

A little bit later my mother and aunt migrated to the kitchen, leaving me at the table, stoned. My Dad and Uncle Rab walked in the sliding patio door from outside and noticed me sitting there. The smell of weed, ever-present in the room, I'm sure is what prompted my dad to call out toward the kitchen. 'Did you get Stacy high?'

"I remember me saying 'no, I'm not high.'

"My dad didn't buy my response for a second."

Getting back to 2006, my grandma was about to make another mistake by smoking weed with her grandson. My grandma was in a good mood that night.

I jokingly said, "Grandma, I just got back from Minnesota and I have some weed. Do you want to smoke?"

My grandma's eyes lit up as my mother's eyes grew darker with judgment.

My grandma looked at my mom and said, "Really? I better not because your mom will get pissed off at us."

My mom changed the subject, but my grandma kept mentioning that I had pot.

My mom would say, "Mother! You're not smoking pot with my son!"

My grandma would say, "You're right! I better not!"

As we talked more, my grandma wouldn't get off the subject of me having weed. She kept dancing around that topic. I could tell my grandmother was fantasizing about Mary Jane.

I might have said, "Grandma! We can go smoke right now. I will pack up as much weed as you can handle. Let's go!"

My grandma burst into happiness and said, "Travis, go get your weed!"

I was shocked. "Are you serious? Let's go then!"

My mom got up in anger. "Do whatever you want! I'm going to change the laundry from the washer to the dryer."

We went below the deck, into the walk-out lower level, and I ventured into my room to get my pipe which was magnificent. It had dark and light blue swirls mixed with oranges and yellows. I showed my grandma the weed as she smelled the bag. I packed up a bowl and gave my grandma the first hit. She ended up torching the whole bowl, holding the lighter to it. She also had a tough time inhaling.

I made the gesture of how to take a bigger hit to her. I packed up another bowl. My grandma took a fat rip and let out a massive cough. It was the cutest thing I had ever seen her do. We exchanged the pipe a few times as I packed up more weed. I noticed my grandma's eyes got bloodshot after a big toke from my pipe. I couldn't believe what was happening!

My mom was changing the laundry, and at the same time, she was furious that her own mother was smoking pot with her son. My grandma was so blazed that she wanted to go back to sit on the deck. By now it was dusk. My mom joined us, but she had a disgusted look on her face.

I don't remember the conversation after, but we sat in chairs on the deck that was lit by tiki torches. My grandma couldn't stop giggling through her bloodshot eyes. I had a smile on my face as big as the state of Alaska. It was a night that I would never forget.

My mom told the entire family about my grandma smoking pot with me. First, my grandma's sister Maud bitched her out.

Maud said, "Dee! That is wrong that you smoked with Travis! A grandmother should never smoke with their grandchild! Shame on you!"

Next, my uncle Jared (my grandma's son) was fuming mad at me. He said, "How could you be so disrespectful as to smoke pot with your grandmother, Travis?"

Lastly, my grandpa called me, sounding disgusted.

He said, "What kind of a grandmother smokes pot with their grandson? Your grandma is one sick puppy, Travis!"

I could tell my grandpa was mad at me as well, so I tried to deny that it happened. My grandpa didn't believe a word that danced off my tongue.

My mom said that she was mostly mad at my grandma for what happened. She cried to her friend Chris about the events that took place that night. I don't regret smoking with my grandma. She has since passed away and smoking weed with her is one of my most cherished memories. The memory of smoking weed with my grandma is right up there with the memories of baking cookies with her in my childhood. It was good to bake with her in childhood and get baked with her in adulthood.

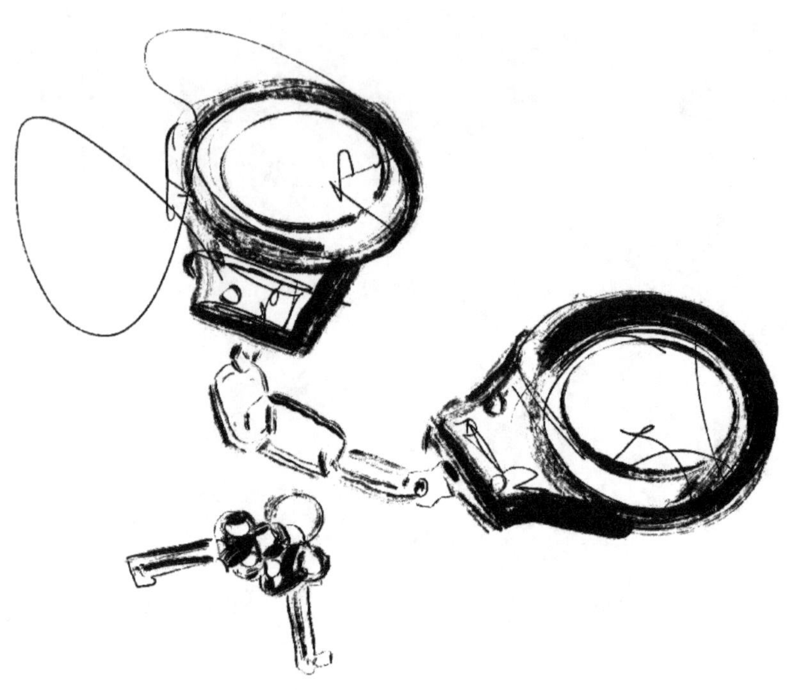

Real Jail

The next year rolled around and Anal Blast was announced to play a metal fest at the Rave in Milwaukee, Wisconsin. I couldn't believe that I would be lucky enough to see Anal Blast for a second time. I finally got a girl that I had been chasing on Myspace to agree to go on a date with me. Her name was Macie, and she would always play hard to get. When she agreed to go to Anal Blast as our first date, I was ecstatic!

I woke up that morning very happy. I was going to smoke marijuana in my closet, but I had decided that I should make my mom happy by applying for a job. I was no longer employed by Pick N Save, so my parents were getting upset that all I did was lay around getting high.

I had in my possession a blank application to Brownberry Bakery, so I scribbled out the application.

I thought to myself, "*Maybe I should just stay home, smoke weed, and make sure that I actually get to the Anal Blast show.*"

I didn't have my driver's license, so I would be risking my freedom to drop off the application. I really wanted to impress my mom and stepdad though, so I decided to deliver the application.

Every time I choose to do the "right" thing over the "wrong" thing, the universe slaps me in the face, which makes me think I should do bad things. On this particular day, the "wrong" thing would be to sit at home getting high all day. I chose the "right" thing which was to be a big boy and drive my 1999 Toyota Corolla to the Brownberry Bakery to drop off my application. The universe decided to slap me really hard that day. After dropping off my application, I saw red and blue lights flashing behind me.

I decided not to stop for the police, which led to a painfully low speed chase. By the time I made it back home, I had eight squad cars following me. I ran into my house, up the stairs, and locked myself in my mom's home office. The police kicked down the door, held me at gunpoint, handcuffed me, placed me under arrest, and took me to the Waukesha County Jail. Needless to say, I didn't make it to the concert that night or on a first date with the Myspace girl.

My mom wouldn't visit me because she wanted to show me tough love. I kept messing up in life by sabotaging myself. My first year out of high school had been a total disaster. Hope raised its head the day my grandpa visited me in jail.

This jail had its own internal Skype system for visits. I was in my jail pod, holding a phone, talking to a camera and looking at a screen with my grandpa's face on it. He was on the other end of the jail with a similar set-up, only he wasn't in a jumpsuit. I was relieved to see my grandfather. He said, "How are you hanging in there?"

"It sucks here!"

He replied, "We're having family talks about what to do with you now. Your mom doesn't want you back until you make some changes, but you can't make changes unless you're out of jail. I want to bail you out, but your grandma says that I shouldn't."

He continued, "I'm going to ask Dorothy if you can stay with me for a while."

Dorothy was my grandpa's girlfriend.

He left me there with a "Hang in there, bud!"

I put the video phone on the hook and went back to my cell. It was a while later that a guard told me that I had been bailed out. It took forever for the paperwork to go through for my release from county jail. My grandpa came with his black Chevy Silverado to get me. I got in the truck, and we drove twenty minutes to his house in the village of Oconomowoc Lake. I was scared because there were going to be no more Anal Blast concerts. I was going to have a lot of growing up to do.

Grandpa's Jail

Things were looking down for me. I was facing a felony charge because of the low-speed chase, and my mom and stepdad wouldn't let me live with them anymore because I was a burnout. What's a boy to do? After I got bailed out of jail by my grandpa, he was going to let me live with him for the time being. This would be a big change for me. My grandpa was far from a role model, but he had always been there for me.

As a young adult, my grandpa had been a brutal biker who ran with an infamous motorcycle club and my grandma was his "ol' lady". All throughout my life, my grandpa filled my head with violent gang stories: tales of lighting unconscious people on fire, pulling a rival gang member's tooth out with pliers, and the biggest story was my grandpa being wanted by the FBI in the early 1970's.

My grandpa never disclosed the whole story to me, but before my grandma's death, she told me that they had to go on the run because my grandpa sliced someone's face off with a knife when he was in the motorcycle club. It was then that my grandpa, grandma, my young mom, and young aunt (3- and 4-year-olds) had to go into hiding in Iowa. They assumed new names and hid out from the FBI for about 5 years.

Eventually they moved back to Wisconsin. My grandparents both decided he should turn himself in because my grandma was pregnant with a son and my grandpa wanted him to have his real last name. My grandpa got his case dismissed because the faceless victim was nowhere to be found. My mom and aunt had a horrible childhood because of my grandpa's choices, but my childhood was lukewarm. I was left with the remnants of the cycle of violence that was bestowed upon my mom and aunt.

When I was a year old, my mom lived in a halfway house in Madison, Wisconsin for 6 months. I had to live with my grandparents during this period. My mom got me back after she got out in the real world again. I spent a lot of my childhood being babysat by my grandparents because my mom was a single parent and worked a lot. In my early childhood, my grandpa liked to play rough with my uncle and me.

My grandpa had a large fool's gold ring. I would be watching Judge Judy, and he would sneak up on me, turn the ring around, and bop me on the head really hard. Another act of love was when grandpa would push me to the ground, put my hands behind my back, and punch me in the chest as hard as he could. He would be laughing so hard.

When my aunt was a little girl, my grandpa had a BB gun and told her, "Stacy, run so I have a moving target to shoot."

My aunt ran screaming and he shot her in the hip. This was in their living room. My grandma was sitting on the other side of the living room and said calmly, "Jeff, don't shoot the girls."

A favorite bonding moment for my grandpa and I was when he would throw an object at me out in the yard. He would grab a board and say, "Now Travis, I am going to throw this board at you, so you need to run away as fast as you can!" I had been hit with so many objects by my grandpa that I had come up with a plan to dodge the next object thrown at me.

I saw the Green Bay Packers wide receivers dart back and forth, so they would throw off the other players. I thought it would be good to run from left to right to confuse him as to where to throw the board. My grandpa threw the board up in the air to hit me on the head. I darted left to right to confuse him. As I darted left and turned right, I ran right under the board as it fell down. It bonked me right on the head. My grandpa was laughing so hard. He told his friends, "I threw the board in the air and Travis tried to dodge the board. He ended up running right under it as it came down! It was so beautiful! Knucklehead!"

Some acts my grandpa did were more fucked up than others. They have made me question what was really going on there. I grew up in Oconomowoc, Wisconsin. The town is filled to the brim with lakes. A favorite pastime in Oconomowoc is to walk around Fowler Lake.

When I was young, my grandpa would grab me as we approached the bridge, hold me over the water, and say, "Travis, I am going to drop you!" All I remember is looking down at my light up sneakers dangling as I looked at a shallow death.

My grandma would softly say, "Oh hon, put him down."

The bridge scenario occurred many times, to the point that when we would get close to the bridge, I would end up running past!

My grandpa always scared all my friends in my teens. When Playstation 2 came out, my grandpa bought it for me for my 14th birthday. He took my friends and I to Blockbuster Video to rent a game for the console. My friend Brian came with my grandpa and me. Once inside Blockbuster, my grandpa turned to us.

"Alright, you can get any game you want, but no games about beating women!"

That statement rattled my friend Brian. Years later, he would still bring up my grandpa's intense energy at Blockbuster that day.

My grandpa had a childhood that resembled the most vile horror movie, so torturing us was his way of being a father figure to us. I will always admire my grandpa, but he gave me an odd upbringing for sure. My grandpa always made our childhood interesting. The weird part was that these acts were strangely out of love.

Girlfriends have told me it was abuse, but it always seemed like the violent acts were just "horsing around."

I feel like the only people who think these stories are funny are my family who lived through this trauma. I told my improv comedy troupe about growing up, and you could hear a pin drop. Nobody laughed and some admitted that it was sad. When my grandma died, my family and I went out to a restaurant. We got on the topic of our childhoods, and someone brought up my grandpa. We told stories about how fucking crazy my grandpa was to us as kids. Before we knew it, we were all laughing so hard that we were crying. I have this memory of my uncle laughing so hard that tears are streaming down his face.

When you live through extreme trauma you tend to laugh it off.

My grandpa is a very tall man, 6'4" in his prime. He has naturally tan skin and very sharp facial features. His eyes are the darkest brown, like a coffee bean, with a glare that looks like he has a sinister story to tell.

My grandpa has some tattoos. On one arm is a tattoo of the motorcycle gang he belonged to. On the other forearm is an outline of a motorcycle that resembled the craftsmanship of a prison tattoo. The engine is missing from the jailhouse motorcycle tattoo. The story he told us is that the guy giving him the motorcycle tattoo was shot while giving my grandpa the tattoo, so the tattoo artist never finished filling in the motor. I don't doubt it.

My grandpa used to be a stud, but he had aged since his hot-stuff days. At this time, he had recently divorced my grandma, so he was a bachelor. My grandpa was in his fifties now and was dating a woman younger than my mom and aunt.

I remember him saying, "I had to ask Dorothy if it was appropriate that you live with us after getting out of the clink. Dorothy is a good woman to let you stay here, Travis."

I had no job, a felony charge, and I lived at my mom's house when I wasn't screwing my life up. I was 18 at the time of my arrest for felony fleeing and my future was definitely not on the upswing. Looking back on my life, I realized it was anything but normal.

My grandpa was still able to pull off being a badass. He had grown out his hair in a long ponytail and dyed it jet black. I made a bet with my grandpa to see who would cut their hair first. We both had shoulder length hair. I think the person who cut their hair first would owe the other person a C note. There was no way that I was cutting my hair first!

I got into his truck outside of the jail. The first thing I said was, "Looks like I'm going to cut my hair now."

My grandpa sighed and said, "Yes, you are!"

Upon my release, my Grandpa drove me twenty minutes from the jail in Waukesha to his house in Oconomowoc. The next morning, we went to Great Clips and they chopped off my beautiful long hair into something more professional. My grandpa didn't waste time with my unemployment; he drove me to every business in Oconomowoc. I filled out 30 applications in one day. I didn't hear back from any of them.

The day after that, my grandpa was in a bathrobe. He was in his pantry stomping Diet Coke Cans.

I asked him, "HEY, grandpa! Can I shoot a gun?"

Without moving his feet, he grabbed a pistol out of the pantry and handed it to me. My grandpa had knives and guns in every room of his house. We went out into his screened-in porch, and I fired the pistol out the door.

Next, my grandpa said, "Do you want to shoot a rifle?" He busted out a rifle, and I shot it off his back porch. The power of the gun firing is something I will never forget.

When I lived with my Grandpa and Dorothy, I often listened to This Providence's "My Beautiful Rescue." I also listened to Kottonmouth Kings' "On The Run'' a ton, too. These two songs were getting on my grandpa's nerves. I was wearing out my welcome.

My grandpa was getting mad because one night I got picked up by my friend Weston and Sarah News.

Weston called me and said, "Bro! Are you out of jail now?"

"Yes, but I'm living at my grandpa's house."

"Bro! I'm breaking you out to get you so stoned!" I needed to get high so badly that I reluctantly agreed to this idea that for sure got me busted.

My grandpa asked, "Where are you going?"

"My friends and I are going out for a drive."

My grandpa seemed uneasy, but he let me go. Weston and Sarah pulled up in his Jetta. I got inside and noticed that they picked me up with this girl named Ariana Freeturn. They all commented on my new haircut. Weston started hightailing it so fast down Pabst Road, and I screamed, "Stop! We're going right past the police station; you can't drive like a race car down this road!"

Weston laughed and said, "Shit! We thought this was a rural town with no cops, so we were racing and blazing bowls. Shit! I'm glad we didn't get busted. My bad!"

Weston handed me a bowl of some flame herb. I hit it and was instantly torched beyond belief. They just smoked me up and dropped my intoxicated ass back off at my grandpa's house. I remember being so scared to head back to my grandpa's because they got me so stoned. Part of me didn't care because I was a drug addict that would do anything to stay high.

When I opened the door, all I saw was a green robe traveling down the stairs fast.

My grandpa went into a rant, "Travis, hanging out with your druggie friends is over. You have a lot of growing up to do. You're 18 now, and you need to be a lot more responsible. You have to look within yourself and find out what you want to do with your life. The party is over, Travis. I can't believe I'm going to do this, but you're grounded!"

I was being grounded at the adult age of 18! It was weird because my grandpa knew I was stoned, but all he did was look somberly in my eyes. After tearing into me, he hugged me tightly, then went back to bed. It was the weirdest experience.

The next day, I had to shadow my grandpa to an AA meeting because I couldn't be alone due to the fact that my ass was grounded. My grandpa bought a rundown limo that he used as an everyday car, so he took his girlfriend and me to a meeting down in Milwaukee in style! I had to stay in the car while they were at the meeting. I remember being really angry about being grounded, but at that time I was out of control.

My next outing as a prisoner was to the Toyota dealership with my grandpa. My grandpa picked out a brand new 2006 white Toyota Tundra. He went inside to talk to a salesman. He was met by one of the many salesmen waiting for their next prey.

I had to sit with my grandpa while this plump tanned guy sat us down in the chairs by his desk. This guy went through the whole sales pitch. My grandpa traded in his 90's black Chevy Silverado. The salesman would type away on his computer crunching numbers, and he would be lying through his teeth about the deal he could give.

My grandpa finally spoke up and said, "Cut the crap! I want the truck for this much with this package!"

The guy seemed uneasy because my grandpa wanted a lot of money off for the new truck. The guy replied, "The best I can do is [blank]."

My grandpa got up out of his chair, grabbed his coat, and started moving towards the door. The salesman probably saw this month's mortgage payment walking out the door, so he ran after the old man. We sat back down with the plump man, and we sat forever working through financing. It was night by the time my grandpa was handed the keys to his new truck.

While he was driving his new truck home, my grandma called to bitch at my grandpa for bailing me out. He told me, "Your grandma asked what I was up to, and I felt like saying that I'm driving down the road in a new pickup truck!"

He wanted to shove it in my grandma's face that he bought a new pickup truck, but he didn't. He also wanted to show my grandma that he didn't need her, but he did! It was sad because my grandpa would do anything to jab my grandma with a good burn. He missed her after the divorce.

Since my grandpa had divorced my grandma, he and his new wife had become swingers. One weekend, my grandpa made me go stay at Sarah News' apartment because they needed my bed for a swinger couple to stay in. My grandpa was going to be doing a wife swap in my bed!

My stay at my grandpa's was wearing on him. He was getting desperate to get my helpless ass back to my mother's house, so he started making phone calls to people in the program that could hire me.

One day, I overheard my grandpa on the phone. "This kid needs serious help, Sid!" He got off the phone and said, "Travis, I pulled some strings and got you a job at a thrift store."

A few years back, an old Piggly Wiggly grocery store was converted into a thrift store in my hometown. Always loving junk, I applied and scored an interview, but I didn't land the job. I was brought into a little bald man's office. The man, looking like a Cabbage Patch doll, introduced himself as Sid.

I was greeted by a red-headed gingery woman named Mary. I later found out that Mary was a psychotic maniac, but for now, she just seemed intense. She introduced herself as the assistant manager of the store. Mary's whole energy at the interview was *very* intense. She asked sharp questions while Cabbage Patch sat back. I was stumbling over my words and seemed like an oaf during the round of questioning by Ms. Mary Bitch Tits.

I remember Mary telling me, "We will get back to you." While she had a "you didn't get the job" smirk on her face.

The interview didn't go well, so I was surprised to find out that my Grandpa had been on the phone with Cabbage Patch himself. The Cabbage Patch man happened to be the father of a girl I wasn't fond of, and the feeling was mutual. I guessed that I wouldn't be in good standing with my new boss, and I was right, I felt a weird vibe from him my first day.

I went to meet with my mom, and she said I could come back and live with them but I needed to drive back to my grandpa's house to tell him. I found my grandpa, in a straw hat, sleeping on the couch. He had fallen asleep with a cigar in his mouth. There was a trail of ash laying on his chest which told me that he fell asleep with the cigar in his mouth when it was still lit. I shook him and said, "Grandpa, grandpa, I'm moving back in with mom before I start my new job."

He was delirious and said sleepily, "Good, good, I'm proud of you." I went to sleep at my parent's house before my first day at work.

First Day On The Job

In the morning, I went to the thrift store to start my new job. Minimum wage was what I was going to earn. I started out at $5.15 per hour. The night manager made $7.50 an hour, so I was low on the totem pole.

The old Piggly Wiggly building had seen better days. It was a big store for its day, but modern grocery stores were getting super-sized. The old structure was big but not compared to the brand new Piggly Wiggly Store they built across the street from their old home. The thrift store had huge round windows on its facade like it was a submarine. It was a faded light yellow color that screamed puke. There was a sunroom in the front that reminded me of a Wendy's restaurant.

Once inside, I was taken aback by the stone-cold bitch Mary. She blankly showed me the donation area. The drop-off donation area was a small triangle room that was once the produce cooler. Once inside the old cooler, I took in a few garbage bags from a car. She introduced me to a hillbilly with his arm in a sling. This fella's name was Buck and he had an oily, ripped camo hat that screamed *redneck*.

Buck looked like he had fetal alcohol syndrome. He was a country bumpkin in his mid-40's. Buck had rugged facial features: the years had not been kind to him. He also had a goatee that was turning gray. His eyes were almost a dull gray, but they must have once been blue or green. Buck's eyes had bags under them from many moons of drinking moonshine. His cheekbones were sunken in from years of substance abuse. Buck had leather skin from the sun beating down on him when he was doing lawn care for a side hustle. He had peppered hair that was escaping from the ripped camo hat because his hair was overgrown like the brush at the side of a neglected parking lot.

Mary took off back to her office. Buck looked me up and down; he snickered after his eyes analyzed me.

"How did you break your arm?"

He laughed, "I slipped on my porch at one in the morning. Broke my fucking arm!"

"Were you drunk?"

He looked me stone-cold dead in the eyes and said, "I don't drink!"

Now at this point, I didn't want to accuse him of being a liar, but Buck looked like the town drunk, so I wasn't buying his stance on sobriety. Buck ended up just being cold towards me.

For some reason, no one seemed to be cordial to me. I met a woman named Emily who was cold to me also. Emily was a short brunette. She was in her late 20's and was stunningly beautiful. She dressed very nicely, wearing a curated look of the most stylish clothes from the thrift store. She gave off that "I wear owl necklaces and have a Tumblr blog" vibe.

Emily went into the sorting area. At the same time a brand-new Super Nintendo, in the box, got donated by a car that pulled up. The way the donations area was set up seemed like I could hide the game system to steal later. The donation room had big makeshift shelves that lined the walls and, I discovered, were filled with stuff that employees stashed to steal later. The security seemed to be primitive, so I lunged for the Super Nintendo, but Emily came back in.

She took one look at it and said, “I better put this somewhere safe.” I knew right then and there that all the employees took stuff home but didn’t dare speak of it!

Next, a lanky Puerto Rican with a headset came in from running the store’s forklift. I soon found out what the headset was for... This guy was rapidly speaking Spanish to girls on a phone dating service for Brazilian women. This was 2007, so internet dating apps didn’t exist yet. The phone-dater said his name was Felipe and he went back to spitting game to his phone dates and unloading a customer’s car.

Felipe wore his black, frizzy hair in a tight ponytail accessorized with his headset for his cell phone, so he could talk hands-free on the phone while he carried in donations.

It was slow that first day at the thrift store, so there was plenty of time to get to know my redneck boss in a sling.

"Where do you live?" I piped up.

In a very rough hoarse voice, he replied, "In Sussex."

Immediately I realized this guy is the town drunk type; he was in his 40’s. It seemed out of place for a guy that age to be working at a rundown thrift store. He was definitely a drinker!

The whole team of employees seemed against me. Growing up, I had an inferiority complex. I would involve myself in things, try to be part of the crowd, but everyone would be scared of me. I always thought it might be the way I looked, but years later I would come to realize that it was my actions and behaviors that scared people.

In kindergarten, my mom told me to be nice to this kid because his parents were divorced. I needed a pencil, so the teacher made him give me one. I looked at the pencil, and I immediately snapped it in half. That same kid would follow me during recess, and I told him to leave me alone or else. He followed me up a ladder on the jungle gym. I got halfway up the ladder and kicked him in the face repeatedly until blood gushed from his nose. By first grade, I had jumped off a stage at my elementary school and viciously choked a kid during the afterschool program. By high school, I had a psychotic break and vandalized the school by tearing banners off the wall. I was arrested for the first time in my life and spent my first night in jail. Until my mid-thirties I really owned the name "Crazy Travis." I just couldn't control my fucking emotions at all. I have struggled with being crazy all my life. These personality traits made my new colleagues unsure of me, especially my Cabbage Patch boss.

That whole week, I met an interesting cast of characters that were the skeleton crew that kept the thrift store running. The thrift store was mainly run by volunteers, but they did have a set of people they paid and could count on. The people I remember that first week were: the guy whose wife drugged him, Donner, Lisa, Agnes, Cookie Jar Jack, and Bugs.

Drugged Man was a very tall, gray-haired man. He had big bushy gray eyebrows with ice-cold eyes. It was like nobody was home when you looked into his eyes. Drugged Man was usually dressed in a torn flannel with a hoodie underneath.

I don't remember Drugged Man's name, but the first thing he told me was that the first time he got head, it was in an apartment lobby from a girl who was in town for the summer as a teen.

"The girl asked to suck all of my guy friends' cocks that summer." He laughed, "My pecker was beet red after she sucked me."

He was the type of old man that you see out in public and you just know right away that he is divorced. He would later tell me that his only wife left him in the middle of the night by drugging him. He woke up to nothing left in the house and months later found the sleeping pill bottle behind the mirror in the wall. At the thrift store he, too, stole everything that wasn't nailed down. Something would come in donations and he would run it out to his car for safekeeping. We'd get a steaming hot pile of garbage like a set of rain boots that the soles were worn down and your toe would stick out. This guy would dash to his car like he just robbed a bank. I could tell Cabbage Patch despised him. He thought that the guy was a geriatric criminal.

Next was Donner. He was a retired firefighter from the nearby Stone Bank area. He also took things home that were donated, but he is still the most noble man I have ever met in my life. Donner was a short old man who had round-rimmed glasses. He was a nice guy.

Donner was at retirement age. He wore big glasses like Jeffrey Dahmer did. Donner was always in a red flannel and a trucker hat. He was bald underneath that trucker hat but had George Costanza-style male pattern baldness that was colored naturally gray. He almost always had Red Man or Beech Nut chewing tobacco in his mouth. Sometimes I would take a dip with him.

Donner had a lot of sayings. "Life is a shit sandwich. Some days you will take a bite of the shit sandwich, and some days you're going to eat the whole shit sandwich."

I would joke with Donner about being old and how he had one foot in the grave and another on a banana peel.

Donner's famous retort was, "When I die, I want to be cremated, so my family can dump me in the toilet, and everyone can piss on me one last time."

Donner was married twice. Donner said when he divorced his first wife, all he had was a milk crate to sit on. He said even though he had nothing to his name, it was the happiest time in his life. He was just glad to be away from his ex-wife.

Donner met his second wife because she was a teller at his bank. She was quite a bit younger than him, and all the boys at the firehouse didn't believe he could get with her. He ended up marrying her and they bought a vacation property in Hayward, Wisconsin.

Donner bought a boat with a guy to share with up at the Hayward property.

The guy said, "I want to see who can fuck their wife first on the boat."

Donner replied, "If you haven't fucked on the boat yet, you've already lost, my friend."

Donner and his second wife had owned a Christmas tree lot that got shut down by the IRS. It was meant to be his retirement job from the Wauwatosa Fire Department.

He would always gripe, "Travis, it takes 10 years to grow a Christmas tree. In the beginning, we would make deductions and pay our taxes. In that ninth year, we got audited. The crop of Christmas trees wasn't ready yet, but the I.R.S. didn't give a damn. The IRS claimed that we were not a profitable business! The dumb shits didn't know that it was going to take one more year to be able to harvest them for sale. Dirty pricks!"

Donner did everything by the book when it came to living in America. It was a damn shame, too, because everyone knows the only way to get ahead is to lie, cheat, and steal. He grew those Christmas trees as a retirement gig for him and his wife, but now the thrift store was his supplemental income.

Once Donner told me the worst story from his years as a firefighter. It was New Year's Eve: a woman randomly met a guy at a bar. They drank until the bar closed. The two of them went back to his place for a one-night stand. The guy fell asleep after sex.

When he awoke, the woman had hung herself on his ceiling fan. The guy panicked and called his lawyer who advised him to call authorities. Her body was going around and around on the blade of the fan. Donner said it was the most horrifying sight he had ever seen. Turns out that the woman was married with kids. She must have needed something different that night.

Donner was a die-hard Republican. I didn't care about politics, so I would always give him grief. He would say, "How do you survive not reading the news?"

I would just shrug my shoulders. During the 2008 Presidential election, I told him about how they made a porno based on the politicians. Donner loved Sarah Palin, so I told him to watch the porn spoof, "Who's Nailin' Paylin?" It was a porn starring Lisa Ann who closely resembled Sarah Palin.

Donner told me, "I'm going to have someone get me on a computer to show me that."

A few months later, we were ripping bags of clothes open and dumping them in the blue laundry bins when he turned to me and said, "That broad that played Sarah Palin was hot in that porn film!"

I still think about Donner to this day, because a lot of the wisdom he bestowed upon me was great advice. I never had a good father figure growing up, so I looked at him like the father he felt obligated to be for me. He saw that I was troubled and reluctantly stepped in to put good thoughts in my head.

Later on, I met Lisa, she was a morbidly obese woman in her 30s that did hardlines. That's the department of a thrift store that goes through hard goods, like knick-knacks and collectibles. Lisa was a short brunette with shoulder-length curly hair. She was very pretty but had a pig face from being bloated. Like a cartoon character, she always wore the same outfit every day. Lisa would be dressed in comfy pants and a black T-shirt. I wondered if Lisa ever washed her black shirt.

She seemed nice, and she also kept stuff that got donated. She would steal items all year from the store and have a big barn sale at her dad's house. Lisa's barn was a well-known spot to get antiques at the yearly sale.

Next, I met Lisa's sidekick. She looked like a porcelain doll. She was a woman in her late 60's or mid 70's. Agnes looked like she was straight out of a page of Archie Comics. She had a bowl cut from the olden days. Her eyes reminded me of Felix the Cat. Agnes had leather skin because she was always puffing on a cigarette out in the back by the compactor. She always wore shorts with a blouse.

She worked with Lisa in hardlines. We piled up boxes of hard goods in a heaping pile. Agnes would go through the boxes in between cig breaks. She was a paid employee of the thrift store, but she came off more as a volunteer. She rode a green Trek bicycle to the store every day because she lived nearby in the old Misty Meadows subdivision.

Before long in the thrift store, I met the man named Cookie Jar Jack. He got that name because he bought and resold cookie jars. He had 3,000 cookie jars for sale in his home. Everywhere you looked in this guy's house, there were shelves with cookie jars. He was, in fact, the guy that would appraise your cookie jar on the PBS program Antiques Roadshow.

Cookie Jar Jack was a short senior citizen. He had gray hair, buzzed on the sides. What was left on top of his head was spiked with hair gel. His face reminded me of an anteater, but a very attractive old anteater at that. He was a yes man, so he always wore the thrift store vest that we were supposed to wear. Nobody else ever wore the official uniform vest at work. Cookie Jar Jack would wear gold bracelets on his wrists to show his status in the antique dealer world. Kind of like the silver fur up the back of a dominant gorilla.

Jack had esophageal cancer, so they removed it. His stomach was up in his chest because of the operation. I asked him if it bothered him.

"Only when I drink Coke; the bubbles tickle my throat."

Jack had a hot rod with blue flames in his youth, so he had a PT Cruiser with blue flames on it as a retiree. Jack was a cheery old man. He also took stuff home behind everyone's back. Cookie Jar Jack would shoot the shit with the volunteers while he was waiting for the next cookie jar to steal from donations. Bob would even steal a cookie jar if he had 5 of the exact same ones. He would never let a cookie jar make it to the showroom floor.

Lastly, I met Bugs that first week as well. Bugs was a shorter gentleman. He had a wild face that gave him features like he was from the north woods—the not-quite-human part of the north woods. Bugs had big, bushy eyebrows to go along with his wild brown eyes. He had peppered hair from being in his mid-40s. He usually wore a baseball cap and was your typical Wisconsin man.

Bugs was a man who lived off his rich wife. He was an odd-jobs kind of guy. He sold bikes on the front lawn of his Pewaukee Lake home. He lived on a busy road, so he would chain 10 or 15 bicycles up at the front of his house with a for sale sign. He claimed to make $2,000 to $3,000 every summer reselling bicycles.

Bugs said, "It's easy money, Travis, because all I do is put my number on a sign out front. When someone calls, I unchain the bikes and get handed cash. I only take bikes that don't need a lot of maintenance. I only want bikes that sell fast and easy."

Needless to say, every bike that came into the thrift store got donated to the back of his truck, if you know what I'm saying. Bugs went so far as to steal Emily's kid's bike that they bought at a real store. Her son wanted to go to his friend's house after school, but Emily made them stop at the store to check with her first. The kids parked it outside and went into Emily's office. In the meantime, Bugs swooped in and copped the cycle. He was an interesting character.

I seemed off to these people. Even to these people. And I definitely was. I needed to win them over *now*, I said!

The demon Mary kind of floated by and suddenly appeared like she was an apparition, called forth by vulnerability. She seemed angry and unstable. I tried to stay away from her. I later found out that she had a coke addiction and was divorced. It made a lot of sense why she was so angry. Mary made jokes after lunch about puking in the bathroom because she had bulimia. After a few days, Mary was gone without a trace and no one heard from her again, but there was still Cabbage Patch Sid to deal with.

One of the volunteers stocked a card table full of day-old bakery items. It was all stale scones, doughnuts, and pastries. I believe that it came from the new Piggly Wiggly across the street. I would take breaks in between taking in bags of clothes to devour the junk food. I would eat it and be like, "This is so gross, but I'm so hungry right now." Stale junk food wasn't the only thing that the employees were loading up on. I found out that every employee stole from the store. If you couldn't walk out the back door with an item, you would lower the price tag. For example, if it was one hundred dollars, you could get it marked down to twelve bucks. If you couldn't just walk out the door with it, the other employees made it happen. It definitely seemed like all the employees were in cahoots against the store! This was my kind of place!

Sid

The more I worked for Sid, the creepier I thought he was. He looked as if he smoked too many cigarettes, and he was a recovering alcoholic. His cheeks were purple from past drinking excursions. He did, however, dress nicely because he was the store manager. Keeping up appearances is important!

Cabbage Patch Sid faced his desk towards the door, so you couldn't walk in on him watching porn. Employees had made the mistake of walking in on Sid watching hardcore Asian porn, and the combination of his doll-like purple face and what was happening on his screen was pretty nauseating. Our location was owned by the Catholic church, so it was strange that he would watch smut there. The store played a Christian rock radio station, so Sid would potentially be stroking it to the very uplifting Christian rock anthem, "I Can Only Imagine" by multi-platinum-selling Christian rock artist MercyMe. The Christian radio station was called The Phish, and it looped on repeat all day while shoppers looked through our aisles. On The Phish, they played Michael Buble's 2007 hit song, "Everything." The Phish also played Michael Buble's hit cover song, "Home." I personally loved hearing this dude sing. These were the only songs I liked that they played.

The station played the same 15-20 songs by the same 10 Christian rock bands. They are as follows: Casting Crowns (Voice of Truth, Praise You In This Storm, and East to West), MercyMe (I Can Only Imagine, and You Reign), Toby Mac (Lose My Soul), Jeremy Camp (Let It Fade, There Will Be A Day, and No Matter What It Takes), Michael Buble (Home, and Everything), Snow Patrol (Chasing Cars), Matthew West (You Are Everything), Third Day (Call My Name), Chris Tomlin (Amazing Grace, and Jesus Messiah), Steven Curtis Chapman (Cinderella, and Yours), and Biggy Daddy Weave

(What Life Would Be Like). All these bands were on rotation while Sid was up in his office whacking his weasel to Asian porn on his work computer. What would the Pope say?

With the thrift store being located in an old Piggly Wiggly building from the 1980s, the second-floor offices had huge round windows like a room from a futuristic movie. One day, Sid had the round window open (which overlooked the registers). As people were checking out, they could also check out the porn Sid was watching. Emily noticed this and ran upstairs to inform Sid of his blunder.

Emily hissed, "Sid! Customers can see you watching porn! Shut the fucking window!"

Sid, the store manager, didn't know how to ring up a transaction on the register, but he knew how to look up porn. Sid, the store manager, didn't know how to close the till at night, but he knew how to search for a mail-order bride. Honestly, I wondered how Sid got the job because he didn't know anything about the operations of the thrift store. He told us that he impressed the board of directors by knowing where to buy the blue laundry bins that held clothes, shoes, and scrap metal. I laughed because anyone could use Google to find out where to order blue bins. Sid seemed a lot like the character Michael Scott from the television show *The Office*. He was totally aloof to what was really going on.

He did not know how to perform any computer functions on the register, like completing refunds or balancing the drawer. Sid just smiled all the time, trying to keep people happy and working in ignorant bliss. He never quite understood what had to happen at the thrift store to make it run, but he trusted us to keep the gears turning. He was in charge but didn't quite grasp his real surroundings. Come to think of it, Sid didn't know how to do anything. He was like a child, lost in the world. Sid didn't know anything about running a thrift store, but because he previously ran a thrift store, they gave him the job. He didn't know how to do anything with donations either.

The only skill that Sid had was to call companies and get them to drop things off or pick things up. He was good at making phone calls to have the dumpster dropped off or a load of bales of clothes picked up. He was a child in a monkey suit playing pretend on the phone. To me, Sid was just playing businessman but not really *being* a businessman.

Sid also lacked human resource skills and was a very inappropriate manager. One time when Emily was sick, she had to go in anyway because, again, Sid didn't know how to use the registers. She was going to go back home and sleep after counting the till, and Sid said, "Oh! You don't have any makeup on today. You look awful; go home!"

The man couldn't do anything for himself. It was proven to me on a hot summer day early on in my tenure at the thrift store. I am not handy at all. I am not a man's man, to say the least, but I have never met someone who was as mechanically disinclined as Sid. He hated my fucking guts, too! Yet, when it came to saving him, I was happy to make a fool of myself to come to the rescue.

Sid came rushing into the big metal door of the donations area.

He blurted out, "Travis, get in my car because I have a flat tire. You need to change my tire to the spare for me."

Sid had treated me like my mother should have aborted me, but here I was clicking my seatbelt in his second car. He luckily broke down close to his home on Summit Ave. He just grabbed his other car to come get his slave, Travis.

I changed the tire for him as we talked about AC/DC's Back In Black album. He drove me back, but he didn't thank me because he is a turd monger. Years later, when he and my grandpa were in a fight, my grandpa made fun of him for not knowing how to change his own tire on his car.

"Geez, Sid! Travis tells me you don't even know how to change your own tire. Jesus! Even my mother could do that!"

Sid looked down at his feet, ashamed and insisted, "I can change it!"

Sid seemed to be a troubled user of people. He had been divorced and he always gave me the "I refuse to come out of the closet" vibe. He had pent-up gay energy, but he was very much into finding a mail order bride.

He would be all mopey and whine to Emily, "How can I find somebody? I'm lonely."

Emily never knew how to answer the questions about Sid's bizarre love life. He had just gotten back from Peru and from meeting a potential slave– I mean wife. After spending 10,000 dollars on fees and lawyers, all he got was a goodnight kiss from his bride-not-to-be. He was now talking to a woman from the Philippines. He spent most of his day not working but chatting with his new Filipino sweetie pie.

Sid treated the employees of the store as lower than dogshit, but at the same time he had a kind heart. He would feel too bad to fire people, so he would make Mary or Emily do the deed. If he didn't like them, he would slash their hours until they couldn't survive working their new measly schedule. I was the employee that Sid hated the most, though.

One time, Sid gave everyone on the staff a 50-cent raise, but gave me a 10-cent raise. Everyone except me knew about the 50-cent raise. I was sweeping, and Sid gave me the news on my 10-cent increase, and I jumped up and down saying, "This is an awesome day! 10-cent raise! Yay!"

Once I became friends with Emily, she would fill me in on how Sid gypped me out of 40 cents.

"I felt so bad seeing you jump up and down for your 10-cent raise because I knew that everyone else got 50 cents."

I knew right then and there that the management and board of directors didn't give a shit about my well-being. I promised myself that day that I was going to rob this thrift store blind for pulling that bullshit pay raise stunt. When I think back on an embarrassing memory like that, I don't feel bad about what I was sneaking out the donation door. Sid treated me like I was his redheaded stepchild that deserved a beating. Little did he know that I would be having the last laugh against him and all my other detractors. I was going to get back at Sid and the board of directors!

Looking back, I'm not mad. I know Jesus needed that extra 40 cents because I was short on my tithes to the Catholic church, and He knew I'd be happy to give it to him. It's not like I needed the money. After all, I was sleeping on the floor in my mom's basement, driving a car with no front windows, and struggling with active addiction. To me, I was living on easy street!

Florida

All the old-timers I worked with would tell me to join a labor union. I was puzzled about why they came down on me so hard about getting a career. I was 18 and living in my mom's basement; that was where the road ended for me, as far as what was possible.

Donner would tell me, "You're wasting your life by working here. You're much too young to be at a job like this. This is a job for a retired snowbird like me."

It was good advice, but I was way too immature to pursue other avenues. I still didn't know what I wanted to do, but joining the skilled trades union wasn't it for me. Deep down, I knew that I wasn't mature enough to join the skilled trades because then the party would truly be over for me. I would have to give up all my druggie friends and start waking up early. I was still sad that my friends went off to college and knew what they wanted to do with their lives, but I wasn't sad enough to join the skilled trades. I felt like life would be over for me if I listened to these old-timers. I thought they didn't know what was good for me even though I didn't know what was good for myself, looking back.

I started to ask customers dropping off donations what they did for a living because I wanted to find a career that screamed "non-conformity." One day, a maroon SUV pulled up. A woman got out of the vehicle, opened her back car door, and handed me a black garbage bag filled with clothes.

I asked, "What do you do for a living?"

The woman chuckled and said, "I own a couple laundromats in the lake country area."

I asked, "Are you a millionaire?"

She again chuckled and said, "No, you have to remember that I get paid in quarters, and the laundry machines always break down. I do alright for myself though."

She left, and I loved the idea of getting paid in spare change while sleeping. Maybe that would be the way I panhandle without begging for it like I told my guidance counselor. That seemed like non-conformity to me, but starting a laundromat seemed expensive and out of reach. A laundromat was a good idea, but it didn't spark something inside me. I took the garbage bag in, ripped the bag open, and dumped the clothes in the laundry carts. Maybe the next car will have my million-dollar business idea.

The old guys like Donner, Cookie Jar Jack, Drugged Guy, and Bugs all looked at me like a charity case. I drove a maroon Toyota Corolla to the thrift store. The driver and passenger-side windows fell down into the door frame, so I'd be driving with the windows down in winter. All the old guys at the thrift store looked at me like I was crazy for driving a car with two broken windows; for these guys, the state of your ride was the state of your soul.

Donner would say, "You really just let it rain inside your car?"

I actually did let it pour rain on me while I drove it. The Corolla had a tan interior which now was invaded by black mold. I used to light firecrackers off in the backseat while I drove to impress my girlfriends. I was trying to make them think I was edgy by risking lighting their hair on fire while driving. What is wrong with me? I am a maniac for sure.

I wasn't impressing anyone at the thrift store. I was slacking off, too. Bugs and I were working together one day. It was slow, and we were just sorting bags of clothes. We were laughing when all of a sudden I pelted a Sharpie marker at his face. Bugs' face flashed into rage as he shoved me against the shelves. The flood of red matched the Sharpie stripe across his nose.

He yelled, "Fuck you, Travis! Sometimes you take shit too far!"

As he had me by the collar, I thought about why I threw that marker at him. I think I was just an asshole who was bored by whatever Bugs had been talking about. I apologized and we went back to sorting clothes. It was a stunt like that which made me a very out-there, degenerate employee. My personal life was as chaotic as the marker toss.

I was partying a lot with my friend Sarah News. I had met her off of Myspace. She had a boyfriend named Weston who was a terrible influence on me. Weston and Sarah were in a very toxic relationship. They would fight constantly, until one or the other was driven into physical attack by rage. Nobody wanted them to be together . . . except Weston and Sarah.

Weston Kulp was a taller guy with dirty-blonde curly hair. He had a slim figure that looked like he wouldn't be much in a fight. His features looked devious. This was a guy who you wouldn't trust as far as you could throw him. Granted, his skinny physique meant you could likely throw him a fair distance. But it would be unwise to trust him that far.

He was a shady character that I called "a good friend." Weston was a very irresponsible guy, which appealed to me as an 18- or 19-year-old who was also irresponsible. I mean, at that age you really don't want friends to be BETTER than you. Weston came from a very wealthy family. His father was the vice president of a very big toilet manufacturer. The company manufactured high-end toilets and bathroom sinks. His father earned over a million dollars a year as the company's vice president. He was a very motivated, successful human being.

Weston, on the other hand, was a human being that had never worked a job. . . his job was breathing. He was the type of guy that lived off of his girlfriend's money. He would just sit around, smoke pot, and play video games.

Weston had just gotten a credit card that had a 3,000-dollar limit on it. Years later, Weston told me, "Getting that credit card with a 3,000 dollar limit made me feel like I was balling out hard."

He started just burning through the card in the most foolish ways. Weston saw a 6-foot bong at a porn store. Sarah told him not to buy it, but one day they were close by the porn store, and he told her to pull into the parking lot. Moments later, he came out of the store with a box that was 6 feet tall. Yup. Sarah flipped out about his dumb purchase. We named the bong "Daddy X" after the infamous member of the stoner rap rockers the Kottonmouth Kings. We would take turns standing on a milk crate to hit the bong. The fact that its size had zero utility, bong-wise, didn't occur to us youthful idealists.

Weston and Sarah were in a vicious cycle of fighting, breaking up, and cheating on each other with people they met off of Myspace. It was during a breakup period that Sarah slept with another guy that she met on Myspace named Justin G. He had a tattoo of the heart from the "In Love and Death" album by The Used. Justin wore black-rimmed glasses that made him look emo but looks could be deceiving. Justin was a very bad drunk who was in disguise as an emo scenester.

One night Justin was at Sarah's apartment, blackout drunk. He was told to move his van off the street because it was winter and plows needed cars to park on alternate sides. Justin left to move his van but never returned. A while later, we discovered that Justin had passed out in the hallway and never made it outside to move his van. He ended up getting a ticket that next morning.

Justin was also unemployed. He never had a dime to his name. Justin would dig in Sarah's ashtray to smoke the used cigarette butts that still had some life left in them.

These were my friends. They were comfortable for me. By this point, Justin and Sarah had stopped fucking but remained friends.

Weston and Sarah had gotten back together again but were constantly fighting. Weston and Justin were partying together and just coexisting.

One winter weekend, Sarah had a big party at her house. Stacy lived in an apartment in her hometown of Sussex about twenty minutes from Oconomowoc. Trucks plowing through town spewed exhaust that turned once-white snow into dark gray sludge. Sussex is a very small blue-collar town. What kept Sussex's head above water is that it is home to the world's largest printing company Quad. The town smelled like fresh printer ink from printing magazines that you would find piled up in your doctor's office waiting room. Driving through town felt like driving through a full-page ad for a blue-collar midwestern town. Everyone in town but Stacy worked at Quad. Stacy worked at a Culver's in nearby Brookfield. Her apartment smelled of cigarettes emanating from the overflowing ashtray on her small coffee table. Marijuana resin stained the walls yellow causing a stench that would make you go nauseous from the tar. Evidence of all the times we were out of weed, and we would scrape her pipes, bongs, and raid the ashtray for roaches.

Like usual, I got too drunk to drive home, so I slept over. That night, Weston and Sarah had a really big fight, like they usually did. The next morning, we all woke up at Sarah's house. Me, Weston, and Justin all sat around a coffee table filled with beer cans, smoking marijuana, and discussing our hatred of Wisconsin winters. As the pipe passed, we kept talking about where we could go, where we could run away to. At first, we talked about taking a trip to Colorado, but it was winter there, too.

Weston realized, "I lived in Florida when I was a kid. I still have friends there whose houses we could stay at."

As we talked about taking the trip to Florida, the talk got more serious. We all decided to move to Florida. Yeah, that's right, we were going to move down there on a whim! I had some money from the thrift store, and Weston was going to live off his credit card with the 3,000 dollar limit. On the other hand, Justin had zero money to contribute to the trip. Justin didn't have a pot to piss in or a window to throw it out of. We felt bad, so we were going to let him come with us, but he had to pay us back when we all got jobs there. Weston had to donate a pair of used sneakers to Justin because his shoes were falling off of his feet.

Our voices grew louder with excitement about moving to Florida as Sarah lay in her bed listening to our insane trip idea.

I remember her telling me years later, "As I listened to you guys talk about moving to Florida, I loved you all, and also, I thought you were all dumbasses. But you were my dumbasses. I never thought you guys would actually do it."

Sarah had to work a shift at Culver's that day, so she left early that morning while we plotted our "big move."

Weston ended up breaking up with Sarah so we could move down to Florida. Justin, Weston, and I headed to my parents' house to break the news to my mom.

"What?" she screeched, "You just got a job and you have a court case! You can't move to Florida!"

I was so not in reality that my response was, "I'll come back to Wisconsin for court!" My mom eventually agreed to let me drive my Corolla down there. I loaded the car with some of my belongings and put a gray and silver tube television in the back seat. We were going to need a television at our new place in Florida. I also loaded up my prized Sega Genesis, so we could play SplatterHouse 2 when we got our first apartment. I kissed my mom goodbye and headed to Justin's grandma's house. Since he had no money, Justin grabbed an acoustic guitar that he was going to pawn once we arrived in Tampa.

So that was kinda the start of the trip. We were just three little hoodlums with a little bit of money and some shit to pawn. We were going to make it an adventure. The plan was to take two cars so we could find jobs easier. Weston was going to take his silver Volkswagen Jetta that he was three months behind on payments for. We took my Toyota Corolla as a backup vehicle. We were moving to Tampa. We planned to leave that night and sleep on the road somewhere. We barely had any money, but we were going to start new lives in a warm climate.

We left that night and didn't stop for the tolls because we didn't have change to spare. It was freezing as we sped off towards the Chicago tollway. The arm of the toll booth came up for Weston, so he took off in his Volkswagen Jetta. I tried to speed after him, but the arm of the toll booth slammed down on my windshield as I almost ripped the gate off chasing after Weston. We stopped in Indiana and slept in our cold cars in the brisk Indiana air.

We woke up shivering in our sleep. We had minimal blankets to use for warmth that night.

We all looked at each other and said, "Are we still doing this?" We all felt that we had driven too far to turn back now, so we drove on.

The next day we didn't stop until Georgia. As we drove down the coastline, all we had was three or four bowls of weed. Since we were in two vehicles, we would meet up at rest stops to smoke the little amount of weed we had together. As we approached Georgia, the climate had become somewhat tropical. Instead of all the grass being dead and yellow, the grass was a lush green. Instead of gray skies, the skies were a light, beautiful blue. Georgia was beautiful, but the people seemed rotten.

We asked several people at this rest stop if they would take a picture of us. Four people all in Georgian southern drawls said, "No." We eventually found one kind Southerner to snap the photo. They took a picture on an archaic flip phone of us with our arms around each other. We were enjoying the summer air, but we still had a ways to go for the part of Florida we had our sights set on.

I didn't know how to drive a stick shift car, so I couldn't drive Weston's Jetta. We would take turns having the company of Justin in our cars. We were driving and I got very horny. I was following behind Weston, so I thought they would never look back. I was so aroused that I masturbated while I drove my Toyota Corolla. I just spurted on my floor mats as I drove my car at 65-70 miles an hour.

We were going to stay at one of Weston's friends' houses the first night. This is about the time that my grandpa got wind of my relocation efforts.

He called me, furiously screaming, "Get your fucking ass back here! I broke my back to get you that job at the thrift store! Don't fuck this up! Make the right decision!"

My grandpa left another message, this time he was even more pissed.

He snarled, "Travis! Get your fucking ass back here! I am going to beat your fucking ass! Alright, I love you. It's Grandpa."

As I passed into Florida, I started not receiving the "I love you's" anymore.

They were violent threats. "Travis, this is Grandpa, I have my motorcycle gang looking for you and your friends in Florida. They plan on beating your friends unconscious and bringing you back to Wisconsin in the trunk!"

On top of that, Weston was getting calls from Sarah, who was claiming to be pregnant. Sarah was a crazy bitch, so Weston recognized that this was her attempt to get him to come back to her. Years later, Weston laughed about our split-second decision to move to Florida.

“We had a lot of forces going against us on that trip”, said Weston. “We had your grandfather saying if you don’t turn around, there are going to be issues, and they would involve blood. I supposedly had a pregnant girlfriend, and Justin was just there. He was just taking up space. It felt like everyone in our lives did not want us to go to Florida. Looking back, we should have listened to them.”

At this point, I felt really bad that I screwed over my grandpa. The thrift store needed me to be there to take in donations. My mom pleaded with me to turn around, but I needed to crash for the night. We made it to Weston’s friend’s house in Florida very late at night. I broke the news to them about how my family felt. Justin and Weston thought it was cool that a violent biker gang was looking for them, but not cool that I wanted to go home.

I bowed my head in embarrassment and said, "I am facing a felony charge in Wisconsin that I need to attend to.” They were bummed and barely understood. Weston’s friend smoked with us before lights out. I remember getting really toasted from his friend’s weed.

His friend laughed at me, "You came all this way just to turn around and go back home? That’s nuts!”

I sighed, “I have court though!” After we smoked, I was shown the floor to crash on. I was out instantly.

My mom called me the next morning to inform me that my grandpa had taken my job at the thrift store, so all was good for the time being. I now planned to have an awesome early spring break! It felt good to know that we weren’t being hunted down by one-percenter bikers. We left Weston’s friend’s house in both cars. Weston lived in Tampa as a kid, so he suggested that we set up camp in nearby Clearwater because it was spring break.

Before we left Tampa, we ditched my car in a factory parking lot. The windows on my car were starting to slip down into the door frame again, but we ended up jerry-rigging them to stay up with duct tape. The factory was old-looking. It had a makeshift grass parking lot with a cyclone fence. I parked my car in the corner of the lot, so hopefully, no one would fuck with it. The factory had a sign that said, "Hiring for 1st, 2nd, and 3rd shift." I knew that if I dumped the Corolla there it would look like I was just parked there for my shift. We headed off in Weston's silver Jetta for the beach.

The next thing we did on the way to Clearwater, and this is probably going to sound bad, but Weston said, "We need to go to the shittiest area of Tampa to try and buy booze."

Weston took us to Martin Luther King Boulevard. There was a run-down gas station in a very seedy part of town. Our hope was that the gas station attendant wouldn't ID us, as we were all underage.

Weston explained, "This is a place that cops won't even go to. We will score booze here!"

Weston, though, was scared to go in, so I went inside to try my luck. Once inside, I bought some beer. I went outside and showed Weston and Justin the booze I bought. They ended up coming inside to buy as much beer as we could get our hands on. We were young and naive, so we bought stuff like Miller High Life, Smirnoff Ice, and Zima's. Throughout the trip, if we couldn't buy alcohol at a place in Clearwater, we would make the far drive back to that shady store in Tampa. We would then make the drive all the way back to our party spot in Clearwater Beach.

Once we got down there, we would go to every gas station to see if we could buy booze. On one occasion, a gas station wouldn't sell to us, so we stood outside asking patrons if they could buy us booze. We walked up to a nice, black truck. A man was behind the wheel with his wife in the passenger seat.

I approached him, "Hey, sir! Can you buy us booze?"

"Honey, tell them who you are," His wife said with a smirk.

The man smiled and said, "I am the sheriff of a nearby county. You boys best leave right now before I bust you!"

I said, "Okay." We immediately scrambled back into Weston's Jetta.

That week, we maxed out Weston's credit card on booze. We hit up the nearest liquor store. We had found the Tampa sweet spot of where to score the liquor, so we were off to the races now!

We drank beer the whole way down to Clearwater Beach. Weston had a mix CD that had the rap song by Birdman and Lil Wayne's, "Stuntin' Like My Daddy." That song became the soundtrack to the trip. We listened to it over and over. We arrived in Clearwater 45 minutes later. All the buildings in Clearwater were a faded pink from the sun. I had never been anywhere like it. Wisconsin was so different from Clearwater Beach.

The first day there, we dug an 8ft by 8ft patch out of sand and made a beer pong table. That brought everyone in the whole area to gather around us, so we met a bunch of people. Through our adult sandcastle, we met some girls who had tequila shots. The girls were feeding us shots out of test tubes and got us excessively wasted.

Weston years later told me, "I didn't really cause trouble, but you know we were definitely there to fuck shit up. The two of us had money for booze, but the three of us didn't have any money for food. We just grabbed whatever we could scrounge up. We ate at the McDonald's on the beach a lot. I remember us getting a large pizza and just splitting that and we'd save our leftovers."

The first day on the beach, we met a Jamaican man that sold rip-off African beads. He would lay out a towel on the sand with beads he made from a craft store. I was interested in how to make my living being a bum, so we walked up to him to inquire about his bead business.

"How much do you make a day selling beads on a towel in Clearwater Beach?" I asked, just a straightforward Wisconsin boy.

He responded in a thick Jamaican accent, "One hundred dollars a day! I make enough money selling beads on the beach to afford a studio apartment in Clearwater Beach, mon."

We thought he was so cool. It gave me hope that I could be a bum and support myself by doing the tiniest amount of work to make a living.

We didn't have extra money in the budget for lodging, so we would sleep under Pier 60. It was amazing to wake up just feet from the ocean. Before I would open my eyes, I could hear the waves crashing on the shore. We slept two or three nights under Pier 60 before disaster struck. I got way too drunk and passed out next to Weston's Jetta. I awoke to police flashlights in my face.

The officer asked, "Where are you staying?"

I was honest and said, "The beach." Wisconsin boy.

He informed us that we couldn't crash on the beach. "I'm going to watch you call a cab to a hotel."

So we obliged. As the cab pulled away with Weston, Justin, and I, we watched the cop wave us goodbye. We told the driver to drive us around the block and drop us back off at the beach. That was the last night we slept at the beach; we were not about to pay for lodging! That was the first time out of three that Weston dodged a DUI.

We needed to smoke weed, so we would stand at Pier 60 and ask strangers if they had any. This mixed-race kid with cornrows said, "I got you, guys. Come to my place, and I will smoke you up."

We went to his place. We were at this guy's house and getting the highest I had ever got in my adult life.

I looked at Weston and said, "I love you, man! I am the highest I have ever been. I love Florida so much."

We left his house so blazed! We asked strangers for weed every day. It got so bad that we asked construction workers for weed who were building a concrete building. They said no, so we asked the construction workers if they could get us a job.

They told us, "You have to join the union before you can get a job." I remember thinking back on what Donner said about joining the union back home in Wisconsin.

I was nowhere near joining a union. We were currently living off a credit card. Weston was maxing out his credit card to keep us drunk. We had nowhere to sleep that night, so we pulled into an oceanside hotel and I laid down my sleeping bag and slept in between the cars in the parking lot. Weston and Justin had the luxury of sleeping in the car.

The next morning, I was shaken by hotel security. They asked in an angry tone, "What are you doing sleeping on the ground?" I was in a daze, so I just shrugged it off, packed up my sleeping bag, and we took off.

We loved cruising the Clearwater strip, and a lot of times we would stumble around drunk. We would just cruise listening to Birdman and Lil Wayne's, "Stuntin' Like My Daddy." One night, these kids approached us to buy them cigarettes. Justin went in first, but they wouldn't sell them to him. I'm not sure why. I guess they just didn't like the look of him. Justin came out and gave me the money. I went inside, bought cigarettes, came outside and was arrested!

I was involved in a sting operation, but I was raised by a lawless biker, so I knew to never admit to anything. This Black female cop had me shoved against a wall by my neck. I was so drunk while she was choking me that all I could do was deny everything and do whatever else she wanted.

"Who were these cigarettes for?" She demanded.

The spirit of my criminal grandfather possessed my body, and I answered, "They were for me!"

She held me by my neck higher and went through all of her entrapment tricks, but I wouldn't budge on my story that they were for me, so she let me go. We were safe once again until the accident...

One night, we trespassed at a rooftop hotel and used their jacuzzi and drank Miller Genuine Draft. The hotel was right by the causeway. The hotel overlooked the bay. The view was beautiful. We got out, dried off, and got in the Jetta. Florida was good to us, but we were being bad to it.

We went downtown again to cause trouble, and it didn't take long to find it. Weston had a marijuana shirt on that looked like the Adidas logo, but it was a giant pot leaf. We used this shirt to attract weed dealers to us. On this night, a very young girl walked up to us with her friends. She had short bright blue hair. She came up to me and grabbed my junk.

"Want to fuck?" She suggested.

"How old are you?"

"I'm 14, but I know what I'm doing," she insisted.

"No way! You're underage! I can't let you do that!"

Justin was hooked and horny though. He asked a question to the jailbait that I will never forget.

He blurted out, "Have you ever seen what a Wisconsin dick looks like?"

Weston was disgusted by Justin's response, as was I. Weston and I turned to each other and said, "Let's ditch this pedophile!"

We took off running away from Justin that night. We went down by the pirate ship docked downtown. Weston and I were so drunk that we climbed on the ship. We wanted to jump off the back of the ship, but we chickened out because we thought that the water could be shallow. Justin found us a few hours later. Only the Lord knows what he did in those few hours.

The next day, Weston was still in his Adidas pot leaf shirt and this beautiful Southern belle approached us and asked, "Where is the weed at?"

We told her, "We don't have any, but we know where to get it! Come with us!"

"Fuck yeah! I'm on vacation with my boyfriend and he doesn't smoke. I'll ditch him and come with y'all."

She got into Weston's Jetta. We were all under 21 and she was 23. We asked her, "If we give you 80 bucks will you buy us as much booze as you can?"

She agreed, so we drove to the nearest liquor store. She loaded our trunk up with enough booze to get a small army blackout drunk.

We then headed to get her the weed she wanted. After a few minutes, the vibe in the car got crazy. We all were excited to be on spring break. As "Stuntin' Like My Daddy" by Lil Wayne played, she flashed us her tits. I remember it getting crazy in the Jetta after she flashed us. We were all on cloud nine as we drove to get weed from this white trash guy we had met previously.

We were drinking and driving with open intoxicants like we always did. We came to a stop light and we had the windows down. It was a beautiful sunny day. Weston took a swig of his beer and set it down in the center console cup holder. As we stopped at the red light, a police officer came through my window.

He grabbed the beer off the center console and said, "Pull over to the side of the road right now!"

He pointed to an area where another police officer was waiting on an ATV by a hotel parking lot. Weston was in his Marijuana shirt and he had the Marijuana Grower's Bible Book by Jorge Cervantes in the back window of his car. It was not a good look. They immediately separated us from our tit-flashing friend. They questioned all of us. The police started accusing her of being a prostitute. The police on our end were accusing us of picking up a hooker.

They were screaming at the girl, "Don't ever get in a car with men that you don't know!"

The police then made her walk in the opposite direction from our car as they watched, so she would be separated from us.

Next, they searched the car and found all the recently purchased beer. They confiscated the beer from us because we were underage. Secondly, they made Weston take a field sobriety test. They put their finger up and moved it back and forth. Weston absolutely failed.

The police officer said, "Weston, I can tell you have had a few tonight."

Weston said, "Yes, I have."

The police officer looked at Weston for a moment, then handed him his keys back.

"Here you go!"

He just let us go! That was the second time that Weston dodged a DUI that spring break. The next day we were getting day-drunk and we parked the Jetta in a spot that had a sign that said, "No parking, violators will be towed." We came back drunk as skunks to an empty parking space! We found out our car was impounded. We had spent all of the cash on booze. Weston was pulling his hair out, and his eyes were swelling up with tears.

He broke down and called his rich parents. Weston's parents wouldn't help us, out of tough love, because of the choices Weston was making in his life. They wanted him to dump Sarah, enroll in college, and get a part-time job. Instead, Weston stayed with Sarah, dropped out of college, and was unemployed.

We found out where the impound lot was. It was in Clearwater, 8 miles away from Clearwater Beach. On the way to the impound, we passed a Christian or Scientology protest. I went off on the protesters.

"Hail Satan! You guys are baby killers! Fuck God!"

That made the guys laugh as we walked in the heat to the tow lot. The worst part was that the impound wouldn't accept credit as a form of payment to get the car out. We were on our own at this point. Weston called his other girlfriend whom he cheated on Sarah with. Her name was Marissa.

Sarah despised her because Weston would always fuck Marissa behind her back. She had humongous tits; they were very droopy breasts that looked like soccer balls hanging in a potato sack. Weston used all his girlfriends, but he used Marissa especially. Weston would call Marissa a butter face because she had big tits with an ugly face.

She wanted Weston back, so she sent the money to us through Western Union. She had to wire us 550 dollars to get the car out of the impound lot. I remember Marissa making Weston promise that if she wired him the money that he would come back to Wisconsin and live with her.

We had to go seven or eight miles to get the wire. There was a convenience store that had Western Union, so we went there. At this point, Justin had not eaten food in two days, and he looked to be in rough shape.

There was a Cuban man who owned the convenience store. We told him our dilemma, and he felt bad for us. He took one look at Justin who looked very starved.

He said, "You boys look like death! You need to eat! I'm going to make you cold-cut sandwiches from my deli here! They are free of charge for you being down on your luck."

The footlong cold-cuts were just what the doctor ordered because the sandwich instantly brought Justin back to life. Once the Western Union came through, we walked back to the impound lot to pay the man. After paying the money, we rolled out with the Jetta.

At this point, we needed to get out of Dodge. When we got the Jetta out of the impound lot, we headed back to Clearwater for more punishment. Weston had maxed out his credit card already, and all I had was $100 left. We wouldn't ever get back to Wisconsin with our $100 gas fund.

On account of having no money the very logical choice was to try to steal gas. Weston and I tried putting a cardboard plate over my license plate with duct tape. We were going to pull up to gas stations all the way back to Wisconsin, fill up, and drive off without paying. We were talked out of stealing gas by our friends and family. We were stuck in Florida for the moment.

Justin had been useless the entire trip: he had no money or food and had gotten us in trouble a few times. Justin had contributed absolutely nothing to us but drained us of money and resources.

Out of nowhere, in one of our bleakest moments, Justin said, "My other grandma lives two hours away from here. She would give us money to get back home."

We were absolutely stunned at Justin's first contribution to the trip! We had Justin make contact with his other grandma. She agreed to lend Justin the money to get us back home to Wisconsin.

We made the trip to a retirement community called Lady Lake, Florida. It was a town that was specifically for retirees. People drove golf carts everywhere. Justin's grandma was a very sweet lady. She was a plump, short woman with short hair. She gave Justin the $300 to get us back home. Once we had the money, we made a very big mistake.

Weston said, "Let's go party one last night in Clearwater Beach!" We all agreed to go back for more punishment, so we headed back to the scene of the crime. Again, we got wasted off beer, cruised in Weston's Jetta, and got another bright idea.

Weston said, "Let's go back to Tampa, so we can party in Ybor City. That is the ultimate party town."

I remember saying, "Let's go!"

Weston pulled his Jetta towards the causeway to head to Tampa. There was a pack of cars leading to the bridge. Suddenly, the pack of cars slammed on their brakes. Weston did the same, but the white sports car creamed into the back of the Jetta where Justin was sitting. I watched in our rearview mirror as the white sports car slowly pulled out, drove across the lawn dividing the street, and left the scene of the accident. It happened so fast that nobody got the license plate of the vehicle.

Justin got out and laid on the ground as I feared that he had internal injuries. The police were called by some bystanders. A couple from New Jersey were so kind to us as we dealt with the accident.

The police showed up to take our statements. This is the third and final time that Weston dodged a DUI. His Jetta was totaled now. We stood on the side of the road frantic because we had nowhere to stay.

The couple from New Jersey came up to us and said, "You're coming to our house to stay with us for the night. We want to help you guys. That wasn't right, what happened to you!"

We got in their SUV and the guy said, "We're stopping at a liquor store, so you guys can drink away your problems for the night."

He stopped at a liquor store and bought us a big bottle of Sailor Jerry's and Coca-Cola. We made mixed drinks as he drove us to their house in Tampa. Justin got so drunk that he started to embarrass us. He started shouting really loud, like drunks do. Justin was not in good form, so I talked to the couple.

The guy gave me some advice that I will never remember because he had gotten me so smashed.

His girlfriend said, "We just happened to be in Clearwater because we are trying to reconcile our relationship. I live in Tampa, and he still lives in New Jersey. This weekend was meant to get him to decide to move down here to Tampa for me, but he is so kind that he always does something like this. He always helps out the less fortunate like you guys. He always puts others before us."

I felt bad, but I was thankful that they were there to witness our accident. We pulled into their driveway, headed inside, and they showed us to a spare bedroom to crash. I was blackout drunk at this point, so my only memory of the night was that their living room was painted a dark red. I remember thinking that the dark color scheme was a bold choice. We crashed for the night.

In the morning, they drove us to the factory where we ditched my car eight days ago. Luckily, my Toyota Corolla was still tucked away in the corner. We thanked the couple and drove to a payphone to call Justin's grandma. We needed a place to stay because Weston had to sort out with lawyers what would happen next with his car.

We drove to a tow lot where crashed cars were kept to get our belongings out of the Jetta. We met a redneck in a flannel shirt with cut-off sleeves. He had a literal piece of straw hanging out of his mouth.

Weston promised the man, "I love this car. I am coming back for it."

The redneck laughed and said, "Son, you will never be back for this car." He was right. That was the last time Weston ever saw the Jetta.

We headed to Justin's grandma's house to stay with her in the retirement community because we were out of gas money again. Lady Lake, Florida was your average Florida retirement community. Golf carts filled the roadways. Fast food joints lined the downtown strip of main street on both sides of the town.

Justin's grandma was really quiet and very annoyed that she had to let us stay with her, but she was too kind to confront us.

It was definitely a weird situation. I'll be honest, I masturbated a few times at Justin's grandma's house. My babies would swirl down the shower drain like the blood in *Psycho*. Showering at her house was my only escape from my current reality. I just wanted this nightmare to be over.

Now that we had spent our gas money that Justin's grandma gave us, she made us do chores to earn more gas money. She made us rake the leaves in her yard. Justin, Weston, and I spotted an orange tree in a nearby neighbor's yard.

"I'm going to steal some oranges from that tree," I said as I went over, took a couple of oranges, and peeled them to eat. As I ate the orange, my eyes swelled because it was so sour. Weston and Justin were laughing as I made goofy faces while I ate the orange. "This orange is so sour."

Moments later, the neighbor came out and said, "Hey, yankees! I could hear midwestern accents from a mile away."

"Would you boys like to try some Florida oranges off my orange tree?"

"Yes," we said in unison.

She grabbed oranges from a different tree than the one I had grabbed to eat. I pointed to the orange tree where I stole the forbidden fruit.

"What is that then?"

She laughed and said, "That's a lemon tree."

I had been eating an entire lemon thinking it was an orange. We told the neighbor our story while we ate oranges in the yard.

She said, "I wish you boys the best of luck getting home."

She eventually went back to her house, and we continued raking up leaves for Justin's grandma. We were working hard to earn back the gas money to get home to Wisconsin. Like the good little druggies that we were, we needed to get drunk and high. At night, when Justin's grandma was asleep, we would raid her liquor cabinet. She had a pretty hefty booze stash. We drank so much of her booze that we had to water it down. Justin found this massive jug of red wine which we consumed and then filled back up with water. I remember Justin being so sick from his grandma's wine. We were definitely living up to our reputation as legendary losers.

Raiding liquor cabinets was not enough, though. Next, we needed to find weed. In the retirement community, nothing was happening with the geezers, but we happened to stop at a gas station where these hoodlums were pumping gas. They looked like something was happening with them. We asked the hoodlums, "You know where the weed is?"

Looking back at that statement now, that was so stupid. We were three white boys pulling up to ask some ghetto gangbangers for weed. I still can't believe that they didn't think it was a set-up.

The ghetto guys replied, "Yeah, follow us!"

We drove to the apartment complex where they were staying. We bought $15 worth of weed for $30 and smoked with them on picnic tables at the apartment complex until 5 in the morning. Our new friends, Snake and Blade, told us that they were members of the Bloods street gang. I find it funny that residing in this retirement community were two hardened criminals from the Bloods. I remember buying weed twice from these boys. I was astonished that we could score weed in a town with all old folks. They both —

Snake and Blade—worked at an old folks home taking care of the elderly. This is America, you know? Unlimited horizons.

They talked to us about gang life and how proud they were to represent their colors. They wore red jerseys when we hung out with them. We ended up hanging out with the gang members two nights in a row and became semi-close with them, regardless of us being a bunch of scalawag white boys.

We probably should have been figuring out a way back to Wisconsin, but honestly, we were just getting high. One day, we got so blazed, we snuck into the Motel 6 pool in Lady Lake. We just swam around like this trip didn't ruin our lives. I did the backstroke and spit out water as I tried to forget about my Wisconsin troubles.

The reason we couldn't make it back was because I was hiding my money in my sock. I didn't want to burn through my thrift store check.

Weston found out and said, "Dude! I'm thousands in debt because of your drinking habit! We need to use that money to get back home!"

He was right, I had to admit, so we used my money to drive us home. Justin's grandma was getting annoyed with us three burnouts staying with her by then. She didn't dare buy more booze, as it would all disappear down our necks. It was time to head back to the Brew City area...

Long story short, I got back. I got a call from my Grandpa. "Travis! I worked at your job, and I loved it! Everybody is taking stuff home! As your grandma would say, 'If it's free it's for me!' Anyway, I threatened Sid so he'd give you your job back since I took your place."

I replied, "That's awesome! Thanks, Grandpa!" It felt good to vacation in paradise and then also get my job back. All thanks to my scary handsome grandpa threatening Sid's life.

My grandpa once threatened a landlord who was jagging my uncle around. My grandpa uses his role in the motorcycle gang to get his family ahead. People get out of his way. My grandpa is so fucked up, but I will always love him. It was around that time that I stumbled across a bit of information that made me giggle.

I saw a national news article about Lady Lake, Florida. The retirement community was awarded with the honor of having the highest rates of sexually transmitted infections in the country. Because they were all old people who couldn't reproduce, people were having sex with multiple partners without condoms, causing sexually transmitted infections in droves.

Supposedly, the mayor had to have an emergency town hall meeting because geezers were having public sex, too. They were catching grandmas and grandpas fucking on park benches in broad daylight. The news article made me smile because I had been there! Hadn't caught any of the action. I wonder if Snake and Blade were caring for folks with crabs and syphilis on the daily.

Daron

When I came back to the thrift store, everyone was very angry that I left them high and dry. Cabbage Patch had a talk with me about my work ethic pre-Florida.

"Travis, a lot of people said you were slacking off when there were no donations to take in. Travis, we don't just work when a car pulls up; if you got time to lean, you got time to clean."

Something hit me then and there. I really wanted to keep this job! I was going to be a hard worker and build a better work ethic!

I went back to donations and there was a guy who looked like he followed the Grateful Dead. He was tall, lanky and had long brown hair that reached down to his butt. The hair was neatly gathered in a long ponytail. He had black stubble on his face, which made him look unkempt. He dressed in a t-shirt and pants that looked like he still had them from high school graduation in 1999. He would brag that he was well endowed, too. He loved to brag about his big penis.

This stoner-type was fidgeting with something on the donations table, along the back wall of the former Piggly Wiggly cooler.

Seeing me he said, "You must be the guy from Florida!"

Just then, Buck walked in and started getting buddy-buddy with Grateful Dead. Buck was like a high schooler acting differently in front of their "cool friends." I didn't fucking care because I was glad to have my cool, unique job back. Buck told me Grateful Dead's name was Daron.

In the time I was gone partying my ass off in Florida, Daron had started doing community service at the store. He was brutally harassed by the small-town Oconomowoc Police during his teenage years, so he racked up $6,000 in fines. He was originally paying off the debt but stopped after he got his license back. The city of Oconomowoc wanted him to pay the rest of the debt.

The fines were mostly from loitering and smoking. Daron had a 5-year license suspension for every charge if he didn't pay up. Daron told the court that he had no money to pay the fine off. They sentenced Daron to 200 hours of community service. Every hour he worked was $10 an hour. Once the thrift store found out that Daron had that many community service hours to complete, they let him work every hour the store was open. Eventually, he completed all 200 hours of his community service and the thrift store hired him on.

In elementary school, Daron had won the State D.A.R.E Bear for an essay he wrote on saying no to drugs. Now Daron looked like he said yes to drugs, and he said yes as often as possible. He was definitely a stoner, but he was trying to work up the ladder of the thrift store. He was a suck-up for sure, but he smoked weed. He had very confusing personality traits.

He had a tattletale energy to him. Daron was acting like he was second in command now, and we were his followers. He was somewhat of a street prophet, on his soap box, preaching the dos and don'ts of helping others. Hare Krishna style.

Daron spoke of reincarnation and his DMT experiences. I saw Daron differently than Donner saw him. To me, Daron was a lot like Charles Manson, and we were his disciples. Charles Manson would intentionally give his followers LSD, and right as they started peaking he would start preaching to them like he was their Lord and Savior Jesus Christ. Daron had given the likes of Donner the acid, but the drug had long worn off on me. I saw Daron at face value.

If a couch with a cigarette burn would come in, Daron would tell us that we had to take it because "someone out there could use it!" He was acting like a board member of the thrift store that would run the Catholic religion like the well-oiled corporation that it pretends it is not. He was now "Corporate Daron". He would be kind to your face, but the moment you turned around he would gossip about you behind your back.

He got aroused off the idea of the thrift store's mission which was: help us, help others. In the Catholic Church, there is the thought-word-deed ideology, which states that our thoughts, words, and actions are all connected. When in a confessional, you need to confess your thoughts, words and deeds to your local priest. In confession, you are told if you're thinking of killing someone, Jesus taught that you killed them. It's like if you think something bad then you have committed a sin. Daron was getting high on the Catholic Church supply.

He believes that life is a simulation. We would get high behind the compactor, but then he would boss me around about how the day-to-day donations operations worked. The problem was that Donner, Bugs, and Cookie Jar Jack would ask Daron before doing donation tasks. Daron lived with his parents and was 35 years old when we worked at the thrift store together. He would walk every day to work. Daron seemed like he was going to be corporate. This was going to be a problem because I needed to have a higher status than Tommy Chong here. Suddenly, Daron was next in line behind One-Armed Buck. I needed to somehow win Buck over so I could be taken seriously.

Willowrun Chalk

When I was a little kid, my Aunt Stacy, who is a dog groomer, told me about the horrors of greyhound racing. I felt so bad for the greyhounds because they were locked in cages for most of their life and forced to race for the sake of gambling. I would always tell my mom that I wanted to get a greyhound, but we lived in low-income housing that didn't allow dogs.

When I was going into high school, my mom bought a condo on Lewis Lane in Ixonia, Wisconsin. This new dwelling gave us the opportunity to get a dog. Now I didn't want to get a dog, but my mother insisted on getting a greyhound. I would fight to the death with my mom about getting a greyhound because I was an unmedicated asshole. I don't know why, but I didn't want a greyhound anymore. I mean, I REALLY didn't want one.

My mom ended up going out to Emeril Kennels (where the adoptable greyhounds are housed in Wisconsin), to pick out a hound. When Willowrun Chalk came home, he looked like an alien. He was very skinny, with a white coat and black spots near his eyes, and had black ticking on his body.

Honestly, I was mean to Chalk at first because I was having a hard time controlling my emotions. I was on and off my meds. During my teen years, I struggled to truly believe that I had a mental illness.

Chalk would hide from me because he hated loud noises. Chalk also didn't like the word "fuck." If anyone said the F word, Chalk would run upstairs into my mom's room to hide. My mom once had a friend over who didn't believe her about Chalk hating the F word. She said to her friend, in a normal voice, "Watch this then. You fucking bitch." Even though my mom said the swears in a calm tone, Chalk got up and left to go hide. He was a sensitive old man.

One day something in me changed. I fell deeply in love with Willowrun Chalk. In a beautiful way, we understood each other. I understood that he hated anger, and he accepted me for being a teenager. I would spend most nights lying in his dog bed kissing him and rubbing his belly. Chalk was the best dog in the world.

My first car was a GMC Jimmy that had no muffler. The truck was loud as hell. If I wasn't home and another loud truck would drive by, Chalk would run to the door and whine for me to come inside. My mom had a friend over, and she said, "Watch this! Chalk, Travis is home." Chalk knew my name and he started to wait by the door for me. When I didn't show, he started crying and whimpering for me.

Chalk was just like me in that all he needed was a good book to curl up with. One day my mom was reading a paperback book. Chalk walked up to her, reading, he grabbed the book in his mouth, and took it to bed to chew on the paperback. Chalk loved to rip up the pages of a paperback novel. From that day on, we would go to rummage sales to buy Chalk paperback novels to rip up.

One of my fondest memories was when my mom and I heard about a humongous fenced-in dog park in Jefferson, Wisconsin. We drove Chalk to this dog park and let him loose. We watched Chalk run. A jogger was running around the fence line; Chalk would run past the jogger to beat him in a race. He would let the jogger catch up; Chalk would take off again. He did this time after time. We watched him and laughed till tears ran down. He was still in his racing prime at that point, so it was amazing to watch him in action, and weirdly touching.

Chalk hated the word, "No!" It was the weirdest thing. If Chalk did something bad all you had to do was say, "Chalk, NO!" CHALK WOULD NEVER DO THAT BAD THING EVER AGAIN! We could leave chocolate cake out, leave for a wedding, and when we came back the cake would be untouched.

One time we came home from a wedding in Green Lake, Wisconsin. It was dark in our condo, and when we turned on the lights in the kitchen, a mouse ran across the floor. Chalk snapped up the mouse in an instant to show us his newfound prize. My greyhound was a mouser!

Chalk was a prestigious greyhound. His mother was Willowrun Becky who was in the Greyhound Racing Museum. She raced in England once. Willowrun Becky raced all over the states, winning all along the way. My dog, Willowrun Chalk, raced at the Dairyland Greyhound racetrack in Kenosha, Wisconsin. Chalk won first place on the day that he retired from the greyhound racing circuit. He retired on his fifth birthday, which was when the owners legally had to stop racing a dog. Usually, if you raced until you were five, it meant that you were a champion. Chalk was our champion.

We eventually moved out of the condo in Ixonia. My mom and stepdad bought a lake house on lower Nemahbin Lake in nearby Summit. Chalk had a few good years with us at the lake house. He was with us for a lot of lake days, eating what we grilled and enjoying time with family. Chalk started to age, getting very gray in the face, even though he was mostly white.

My stepdad insisted on getting another, younger dog. He chose a Shorthaired Pointer/Coonhound mix named Bell.

Chalk hated Bell.

My mom has dated some big assholes who insisted that greyhounds didn't act like real dogs, so they forced my mom to get a "real dog." Men want dogs that play fetch, drink out of the toilet, and eat their own poop. Chalk didn't do any of those things because he was classy. In his last few years, he was bothered by a young pup that wanted to wrangle him up. Chalk was old and tired. One day, Chalk started to not feel very good.

The night before and the aftermath of Chalk's death were a blur for me. My mom remembers that tragic day best because he was her dog after all.

My mom recalled the following:

"Chalk wouldn't eat his food and barely got out of bed. I became really worried when I made chicken for him, and he wouldn't even eat that. I knew something was very wrong. I called the vet and got an appointment for later that day. When you came home, I told you to go in my room and hang out with Chalkie because he wasn't feeling well. You laid in bed with him. As you got ready for work at the thrift store, I asked you if you wanted to come to drop off Chalk at the vet. Your response was that you would see Chalk tomorrow; you then took off for the thrift store.

"I think we were all in denial about how sick Chalk really was because we loved him so much. Before Chalk got in my car to go to the vet, he stopped and took a dip in his swimming pool which gave me hope that he was going to be ok. When Dr. Laurdison entered the room, he said he could smell that Chalk was toxic and was most likely in liver failure. He said he needed to keep him to run tests and give him liver medication through an IV to improve his liver function. I got a call from Dr. Laurdison a few hours later saying that the problem was in fact Chalk's liver and that he needed to be on IV overnight, but that I may want to consider putting him down if the medication didn't work.

"I was getting ready the next morning to pick my dog up when I received a phone call that Chalk never made it through the night. My whole world shook that day. I was beyond devastated. I kept begging the vet to let me see him. They said no that I wouldn't want to remember him that way. I dreaded having to wake you up to tell you that Chalk died. The rest of that day is a blur, so I don't remember everything. I do remember telling you that you didn't have to go to work, but you wanted to try to go in. I do remember that your Aunt Stacy found out because she had a vet appointment for her dogs at the same clinic. When she went in, she asked the vet how Chalk was doing, and they told her that he passed away and that I kept calling begging to see him. They asked Stacy to bring Chalk's collar and leash to me. Aunt Stacy came over that day with Chalk's belongings."

That morning when my mom told me that Chalk died, something died inside me. I felt empty inside and changed my mind about going in. I phoned the thrift store and asked for Buck.

His raspy voice eventually answered, "Hello."

I replied, "Hey Buck, it's Travis. Look, my dog just died. Is there any way that I could have off today? I am just really bummed out."

He paused and laughed, "You want off because your dog died? Man, you got to come to work today!"

I am a very passive person, so I just agreed to come in to work that day. Buck was such a drunk fucking prick to not give me the day off. Chalk was very special to me, and Buck just mocked me for being sad about my animal dying. Fucking douche!

I went to work that day and took in donations like an emotionless robot. I remember being very low energy. I wasn't my normal psychotic self; I was just nothing. I don't remember if Buck apologized that day, but part of me thinks he didn't. I took off in my

Corolla with no windows, and the black mold interior, in a very somber mood. I thought about Chalk all day at work.

I still think about Chalk a lot. When he died, my stepdad said, "We will never meet another dog like Chalk in our lifetimes. He was one of a kind." I still think of what my stepdad said because he was absolutely right. . . One of a kind. He fit right in in our family. He had a horrible life at the track so he could be sensitive. He had his quirky ways of doing things. He could be wary of others but formed strong bonds with those he trusted. He saw prey and went after them. He was a Geier!

BEER
MILWAUKEE

Drinking With Buck

That summer, the board of directors wanted the floor of the thrift store stripped and waxed. It was going to take all summer because we could only strip and wax the floors on a Saturday. After all, the store was closed on Sunday for a day of religious observation. Buck, the one-armed redneck, was going to force me to spend Saturday nights alone with him stripping the floors.

Stripping and waxing the floors with Buck was mundane at first. We would work our regular Saturday shift, then when the store closed, we would move all the furniture to one side to work on the floor. Buck would crank 70's rock and sing to himself while he used the buffer. I would stand and hold the electrical cord while he glided along with the big buffer. Buck was always kind of rude to me, but this one night while stripping the floor, we became as close as my hatred for him would allow.

I don't know what was said, but at one point getting beer was mentioned, and the cut-off time for beer sales in Wisconsin was quickly approaching. The more beer was discussed, the more Buck's ears perked up. Beer was on Buck's mind as he became infatuated with the liquid. Buck was out the door before you knew it. He headed to the fancy new Piggly Wiggly across the street and reappeared with a 30-pack of Miller Genuine Draft. We got fucking obliterated drunk at the religious thrift store that night. We got so drunk that it was making it challenging to focus on the floors.

Instead of singing the words, we were drunk shouting the words to the 70's hit songs on the radio.

"THE BOYS ARE BACK IN TOWN! THE BOYS ARE BACK IN TOWN!" We shouted as Buck tried to slide the buffer around.

At one point, around midnight, he called Daron. Buck was leaving messages on Daron's voicemail. He was so slushy drunk that he was slurring his words as he rambled on during the voicemail. That drunken night, Buck told me to drive drunk home safely, and I ended up making it to my parents' house without committing vehicular suicide or homicide.

Daron was suspicious the next time I saw him at work. Daron was the kind of guy that was out to knock you down a few pegs on the thrift store totem pole so he could get hours. He pulled me aside and said, "Were you guys drunk at work this weekend?"

I laughed and said, "No!"

Daron looked skeptical, "Oh yeah? Then why did Buck call me drunk at midnight telling me to bring some weed to the store?"

I giggled in my head as I lied through my teeth to Daron. Now that I was witness to Buck's drinking ethic, I couldn't help but notice he drank all the time during work at the store. Daron would catch him drinking out of a flask when he thought he was alone in the donations room. Buck would always bring a road soda to work, something he could pass off as a regular soft drink. Daron would catch Buck spiking his morning soda with his flask. The thrift store put up with Buck's drinking, and they always gave him a second chance.

After all, Peter came to Jesus and asked, "Lord, how many times shall I forgive my brother or sister who sins against me? Up to seven times?"

And Jesus answered, "I tell you, not seven times, but seventy-seven times."

My question is, does that verse account for drinking at work?

Understanding Differences

I had two bullies in middle school that actually did me a favor by being mean to me. One kid was named Sam Weeden and the other was Ben Sixteen. They both hung out together, listened to hippie jam bands, and were both classified as "sweet kids," which was a term for popular jock assholes that listened to hippie music. Another criterion in the "sweet kid" starter pack was that you had to be involved in The Young Life Youth Group.

Ben and Sam would ridicule me for wearing pro wrestling shirts to school. I got picked on to the point where I hated all people. Sam and Ben wore Grateful Dead and Phish shirts to school, smoked pot, and were just douchebags.

Both Sam and Ben had the same interests; one being that they loved to ski during the winter. Ben was short and stocky with a buzz cut at the time. He was just an edgy prick. He gave off very bent energy for a middle schooler. Ben was the first kid I heard of who drank beer in middle school. He dated all the popular girls at our school. Whatever the fuck "dating" meant to a middle schooler, Ben had it in spades. They would pick on me during gym because I loved Ozzy Osbourne.

In middle school, Ben and Sam would make us listen to the same Steve Miller band mix tape every morning for our gym warm-up. All the other outcasts and I who listened to metal demanded that they play Ozzy. My group of friends were the kids who didn't try during gym class. I was in the group that would stroll the court during a gym-class basketball game. This was the year before *The Osbournes* show had come out, so Ozzy wasn't TV's most lovable dad yet. My gym teacher thought that Ozzy was still a bat-eating devil worshiper. My friends and I made my gym teacher let us warm up to the Blizzard of Ozz album. The outcasts finally beat our stoner rock nemeses Sam and Ben.

On one occasion, I wanted to be the leader of the group that I was in for Social Studies. Sam wouldn't let me be the leader, and he picked on me super hard about it. I had a Walter White moment where I just snapped. I felt like all the good I wanted to do in the world had been pissed on by Sam. I went home from school in a homicidal rage.

I started screaming, "I'm going to go to school tomorrow and I'm going to stab Sam to fucking death!" I also screamed all night, "I'm going to shoot up the school tomorrow just like the boys at Columbine!"

My mom was so scared that she called my therapist, Ned Schwartz. He ended up having me committed to Milwaukee Psychiatric for my mental breakdown.

In high school, Sam and Ben played in hippie jam bands together, got hot girls, and smoked tons of weed. In high school, I was a psycho. I had an episode at school where I kicked over trash cans and ripped down banners. A cop tackled me and arrested me on the spot. I ended up serving a year of court-appointed probation for it.

I served the year of probation and had arranged a smoke fest for my release from supervision. Somehow, the group I was with met up with Sam and Ben. We all drove in my black GMC Jimmy for a smoke session. The road was spinning as I drove; I was so high that I was almost hallucinating. I got way too high to drive, and I needed to pull over.

As I got in the passenger seat of my own truck, I was relieved to not be driving. Sam got behind the wheel. I had made up with Sam because he was a true hippie now, so he was all about peace and love. I was so high that I started to have a back-and-forth with

Sam. About 10 minutes went by and I turned and looked at who I was talking to in the driver's seat and it was skeevy Ben Sixteen!

I remember meeting eyes with Ben Sixteen and recognizing his dead-inside state. I was so disgusted that he was driving my pride and joy which was my 1994 GMC Jimmy. The whole time I had thought it was Sam who was driving! I had been just chit-chatting with Ben who loved hippie jam bands, but he was not about peace and love.

Upon graduation, a lot of the jam band hippies from my school moved out to ski resorts in Colorado to live in the dorms, ski at the resort, and party their asses off while earning a little money by working on the mountain. Sam later joined a band called The Giving Tree Band which was very successful. They had a great song called "Circles."

Ben had been no different than all of the other hippies that went to Oconomowoc High School. At this time, he had goopy dreadlocks and was following Phish around the country.

Ben met a girl from Peru that he fell madly in love with. They dated all throughout the ski and snowboard season. When the resort closed for the season, his girl moved back to her native Peru. Ben was a puppy in love at this point. He decided to move home, get a job, and save up to move to Peru to be with her. That is how Ben Sixteen, my high school bully, ended up working at the thrift store.

He needed to save money to make trips to visit his sweetie. When I first saw Ben Sixteen at the thrift store, I thought my worst nightmare had come true. My bully was here to destroy me! He seemed very different though. Being an adult in the world had changed him. He had gotten some culture under his belt. Leaving the politics of being popular in high school had changed him, too. Ben was kinder now; he was definitely obsessed with this woman from Peru. Ben was even learning Spanish to be more accepted by her family.

Because I was working full-time at the thrift store, Ben definitely looked to me for guidance. Suddenly, I had the power and was in control. Ben was turning out to be a totally different person than the one from high school. We would smoke a little weed together at the thrift store when it wasn't busy; we were really getting to know each other. In between unloading cars of their endless garbage bags of clothes, Ben spoke of his trips going down to visit his girl in Peru.

He said, "Travis, it's crazy, I got on a bus in Peru, and because I was American, I was kicked off the bus! They definitely have it out for Americans who come to their country."

I was starting to become fast friends with Ben as he worked to save money for trips to Peru that summer. On one occasion, he blasted the DJ BassNectar through his car speakers. I remember looking at him on a beautiful sunny day just blaring this EDM music and talking about the life and times of the DJ BassNectar.

Ben would also always tell me to listen to Alyson Krauss and Union Station. He would hound me to listen to her. He was kind of all over the place on music choices. After the summer was over, Ben headed out west again to meet his Peruvian Queen at the resort. When I was 20, on Halloween, I saw him at a Bassnectar concert at the Miramar Theatre in Milwaukee, Wisconsin. The day and night were something out of a nightmare. I drank a bottle of Sailor Jerry's and smoked some really good weed with this drug dealer that I was friends with from my days of going to local Wisconsin metal shows. I got so wasted and stoned before the show that it was hard to function.

This would mark the last night of my life that I ever drank alcohol. I sat in a theater chair and was trying to keep the room from spinning when I was tapped on the shoulder by dreadlock Ben. I still worked at the thrift store, so we had a lot to catch up on. As I was annihilated drunk, I tried to pay attention to Ben. I really tried to be in the moment, but I couldn't function. It was really loud in the concert hall, so there was a lot of nodding to Ben even though I didn't understand a word he said. We shook hands, and I never saw him in real life again. I have looked him up on Facebook a few times though.

He eventually cut his dreads, moved to Peru, and got a real job. Years later, he and his now-wife moved to Wisconsin. Ben ended up having a few children with his Peruvian lover. One time, I posted on Facebook that I loved Alyson Krauss and Union Station. My aunt had just gone to her concert and burned me a CD of hers. When I made that post, Ben replied in the comments, "Finally." That comment made me smile.

I loved working at the thrift store with my old bully Ben Sixteen that summer. It really goes to show that life is never what you expect. I had no idea about the real relationship that I would have with my old adversary from high school. It just goes to show you that you should always give people a second chance. You never know what could sprout from a rotten core. Sometimes a rose blooms.

The Carpenter

One of my favorite bad boys who had to do community service was this scrappy dude named Rob. He was a short guy with a big full blonde beard. He was in his mid-30s, but he acted like he was my age. I was in my very early 20s at the time. Rob was working off a DUI. In those early days, all I lived for was going to hard rock and heavy metal shows. Rob was no different. He and his friends went to every heavy metal show in the Midwest that they could buy tickets for. His favorite artist to see was Kid Rock; Rob told me the best show he ever saw was Kid Rock at the Eagles Ballroom.

"Kid Rock played for three hours straight with no opener, dude! He played every song you would want Kid Rock to perform."

I thought to myself, "*I would never want to be caught dead at a Kid Rock concert.*"

Rob was a non-union carpenter, so he could definitely afford the tickets to all the metal concerts around town. I liked his style of blue-collar work and thought maybe this is what I should do with my life. All my friends were off at college partying, and spending a fortune to study, but the carpenter was off partying and getting paid good money to hump drywall for a living. I wanted to be like him: a scrub that worked hard and played hard. I loved how he seemed like he was always high. I wasn't ready to learn a skilled trade though, so I continued asking cars that would pull up what they did for a living in hopes they would tell me, "I'm a working class rockstar." The carpenter was a working class rockstar that had fallen on hard times.

He would come in to do community service on Saturdays to work his time off. We would vibe about metal music and our love for marijuana. On a few occasions, he brought weed to smoke with me.

We would go by the compactor to take tokes off his one-hitter that he kept in a dugout. While Rob took in donations, he would drink. Looking back, he was an alcoholic who was struggling to get sober. Now that I'm his age, I can totally relate to his substance abuse. I spent years struggling with substances. In a weird way, I ended up living the life that he led. I kind of grew up to be just like him.

One Saturday, he came back from seeing a concert in Florida. He drove this beat-down ratty truck. The truck frame had cracked in half while Rob was in Florida. He took the truck to a shop, but they didn't want to let Rob leave with the truck.

The mechanic told him, "It would be a liability for us to have you drive this truck back to Wisconsin."

Rob demanded that they release the truck. He ended up throwing a fit until they let him drive off with the truck. He left with the truck back to Wisconsin.

"Every state I passed, I would pull over to check the truck's frame to make sure I wasn't going to die in a fiery crash."

Eventually, Rob finished all his community service hours. He brought weed in one last time to smoke with me.

He said, "I'm actually going to miss doing community service because of you, Travis."

I was touched by that! It's weird that I never forgot about Rob. I sometimes wonder why he is a big memory for me. Maybe it's because I ended up struggling with addiction for most of my 20s and 30s. Rob always seemed like he was running from something. I always wondered what he was running from, but then through my own struggles with substance abuse, I realized he was running from himself.

The Letters

Daron and I were in the thrift store warehouse building a giant city of used furniture. The furniture would get piled up to the next level of the furniture skyscraper. We were climbing up on a table that was stacked up. Then we would hoist it up to the next tier until we were at the top. OSHA would have been so proud!

Suddenly, my grandpa showed up again at the store. He said, "I really miss working here, Travis! I miss all the free shit. I really want Buck's job when he screws this good gig up."

"I don't know if they'll let Buck go. You might have to take a donation attendant job like me."

"No, I'm going to be your manager, Travis."

"Why are you here?"

He smiled. My grandpa previously worked at the thrift store, so he knew everyone I worked with. He had everyone write a character letter to the judge about me because my sentencing was coming up. My grandpa collected letters from most of my coworkers so I could beat this felony charge for evading the police in the low-speed chase. Sid, who hated me, even had Emily write a letter as him. I was touched!

My mom had a hard time finding a lawyer who could guarantee that I wouldn't do jail time. One attorney told my mom, "The best I could get your son is six months in jail." It was looking grim until we found this lawyer out of Waukesha named Joseph Dorelack. He informed my mom that he could get me just probation for the felony fleeing charge. My mom's friend Chris gave my mom the money to retain Attorney Dorelack.

Joe suggested that I get into counseling. His next suggestion was to gather up character letters from people I worked with, were friends with, and family members. The sentencing was fast approaching, and I was about to find out my fate for not stopping for the police.

At court, the judge looked me in the eye and said, "After reading these letters, I know I'm never going to see you in here again. People speak very highly of you." Tears were welling up in my eyes as I heard the judge hand down the sentence of two and a half years of probation. I was so happy to not spend any time in jail.

This was the second time in my adult life that my grandpa had gone above and beyond to save my raggedy ass. It scares me being a parent now because I don't want my sons to make all the dumb mistakes that I made. My grandpa saving me those two times definitely gives me inspiration for how to parent my children. I just hope I never have to collect letters for my sons to give to a judge.

Give Him Rope

My grandpa called me at the thrift store; I answered the call on the phone hanging in the donation center.

"Travis, I want Buck's job as the donations manager. I miss taking shit home. If it's free, it's for me. I need my junk, Travis! How's Buck's drinking been?"

I said, "Buck hasn't shown up the past several weekends because he's been on drinking binges. Grandpa, the worst part is that Buck was supposed to open the store, so all the employees were locked out. We were all left standing there with customers wondering what was going on."

"They're never going to fire him, Grandpa. This is a religious thrift store; they'll keep giving Buck chances. Good luck sliding in as the donations manager!"

I will never forget my grandpa's response: "Travis, mark my words, Buck will hang himself. You just have to give him enough rope. They won't put up with Buck's drinking much longer because they have a business to run."

The board of directors claimed to be holy rollers but they would habitually enable Buck by giving him chances after drinking binges. The board didn't understand addiction even though they helped addicts get back on their feet by giving them free furniture through the church's voucher system.

Two weeks later, Buck did not show up again; Sid and the board of directors decided to let him go. Sid came to have a smoke because for some reason we smoked in the donation room.

Sid sat down and said, "We need a new donations manager; you guys know anyone?"

I said, "My grandpa's been a blue-collar worker his whole life, so he knows how to use the bailer, forklift, and how to load a semi. You need to hire him!"

I could see the rusty gears turning inside Cabbage Patch's brain. The cobwebs were being torn down by the gears. We might just have a non-porn thought from Cabbage Patch!

He said, "That just might work! What is your grandfather doing for work right now?"

I said, "He's driving quad axle dump trucks, but he'll come to work here! I'll call him right now!"

I dashed to the phone in the back warehouse, dialed my grandpa, and heard, "Hello."

I said, "Grandpa! Call the store right now because Sid wants to hire you as the donations manager."

He got off the phone and called the store to speak with Sid. Cabbage Patch came back and informed me that my grandpa had scored an interview. My grandpa was hired that next week and put in his two weeks with the dump truck company. Hell was about to freeze over. The Geiers were in charge now!

Grandpa In Charge!

When I was a child, my mom would drop me off at my grandparents' house. My grandpa would be waiting for me in the driveway. The first words out of his mouth would be, "I got a job for you." I would then spend the rest of the day pulling weeds or some other back-breaking job. My grandpa clearly misunderstood child labor laws.

Flash forward to my grandpa's first day as my manager at the thrift store. I came into the donation area to start my morning. My grandpa came through the double doors wearing the blue vest that we were supposed to wear.

My grandpa took one look at me and said, "I got a job for you."

I laughed and thought, "*Some things never change.*" I spent the rest of the day doing manual labor. He had me reorganizing the whole back warehouse and store to have it the way my grandpa liked it.

The second my grandpa was in power, he let it go right to his head.

"Travis, we are going to rob this place blind!"

I agreed because of how they treated me with the 10-cent raise while everyone else got a 50-cent raise. I thought to myself, "Fuck this place!"

My grandpa and I weren't the first ones to rob the store blind because of management's idiocy. When the thrift store first opened, they hired a girl named Izzy who was a grade lower than me in school. She embezzled a ton of money by doing returns:

giving fake refunds to customers that didn't exist. The old manager Mary caught on, and Izzy was fired. You would think that they would have learned to tighten up security. Right? Nope!

I don't know why Sid would trust my grandpa, on account of him being a menacing gang member in his younger years. On the first day of the reign of Geier, my grandpa wanted to fire every old guy that worked in donations. My grandpa hated all the old guys except Donner. Everyone loved Donner because you could tell he was an honest, hardworking man.

My grandpa told me, "I'm going to fire the Cookie Jar Man! All he does is shoot the shit with the volunteers and wait for his next cookie jar to come in."

I told my Grandpa, "We need workers, we get a lot of donations every day."

My grandpa walked up to Cookie Jar Jack and said, "I'm sorry, Jack, but I'm letting you go!" Jack had a disgusted look on his face. He knew what was going on.

Bugs perked up and asked, "You're not firing me too, are you?"

My grandpa pondered that for a moment and said, "Why, yes I am, Bugs!"

Both guys got their stuff and left in anger. Bugs left muttering obscenities under his breath, cursing out my grandpa.

Cookie Jar Jack was a class act, because he left the store saying, "It was fun while it lasted, but I won't work a second longer for your grandpa." I smiled at Jack and wished him luck.

I loved working with Cookie Jar Jack because we made work fun. Cookie Jar Jack would buy us Taco Bell, and I would drive to pick it up. I would come back with his order, but I would get him like 100 packets of hot sauce.

He would tell me, "The price of Taco Bell is going to go up because you grab a ridiculous amount of hot sauce packets."

As time went on, I would grab more and more packets as a joke. One time, I came back with two handfuls of packets. I was going to miss him for sure. I went back inside knowing that I would never see Cookie Jar Jack again.

Once inside, My grandpa turned to me and said, "Now, what are we going to do, Travis? I just fired everybody!"

My grandpa still jokes to this day about how Bugs fired himself that day when Bugs asked if he was fired too. My grandpa just said yes because Bugs was stupid enough to ask the question. My grandpa wanted me to reach out to some of my buddies from high school to work at the thrift store, but they had all moved forty minutes away, to Milwaukee. We were definitely in a bind now, but my grandpa did it because he didn't trust them. My grandpa wanted to start stealing a lot without the watching eyes of those who had investments for themselves, like cookie jars.

Later that day, I smoked marijuana with Daron who Sid insisted that we keep employed. I mentioned to Daron while we smoked that I just got put on probation.

He asked, "Who do you have?"

I replied, "Vance Tut."

His eyes lit up. "You have the worst probation officer in Waukesha County. He has the highest revocation rate of any probation officer in the county. I heard stories that he once revoked someone for going on a family vacation. I also heard he would show up on garbage day and go through your trash to find weed, seeds, and stems. You're fucked, dude!"

I was fucked on both fronts: life and work. Daron, my grandpa, and I would have to put in double duty to take in all the donations. We would figure out a way to make donations run for the time being.

Later that week, I was smoking pot again with Daron by the dumpsters when I heard my name over the intercom. "Travis, you have a phone call on line one."

I thought it might be my mom or my girlfriend, so I casually answered "Hello." It was my probation officer Vance!

"Travis, we need to talk."

I gulped, "Okay."

Vance continued, "My computer system is telling me that we need to do a home visit." I laughed inside because I knew he worded it that way to catch me off guard. He thought I might slip. I might refuse.

"Great!" We set up the appointment. At this point he was a major buzzkill to my feeling of euphoria. I hung up the phone and went back to the donation area to find my grandpa.

My grandpa was becoming quite the celebrity around the thrift store. Employees started to take their cigarette breaks in donations to hear my grandpa's wisdom. My grandpa started to tell old Native American stories to the employees about how he grew up on an old Indian reservation.

My grandpa was fighting dirty with all the employees that stood in his way. He would try to get Emily in trouble at work by telling Sid about stuff she did during the day. My grandpa would also test the waters with Emily to see what he could get away with not doing at the store. If my grandpa could get away with being lazy, he would blow off Emily entirely and avoid her.

My grandpa would try to get away with not doing his job duties anytime that he could. The only thing he would listen to, from Emily, when it came to the store, was keeping the payroll down in donations. If there was a task he specifically was accountable for, he would follow through, so as to not bring attention to himself, but other than that my grandpa was a stone-cold slacker.

My grandpa would try to pry into Emily's life, asking questions about her family, so he could use her past against her. He would tell an old Indian story to Emily where he would manufacture the moral of the story to cater to Emily's current dilemma. He would tell these old Indian stories where the moral of the story would imply that Emily had a fucked-up life.

Everyone at work thought that my grandpa was so interesting. My grandpa called himself Ten Bears which was supposedly his Native American name. All my life he spoke of how he was native and grew up on the reservation as a teen. He claimed to have grown up on the reservations around the Crivitz, Wisconsin area. As a kid, my grandpa always spoke of building huts and teepees, and I ate it all up. I told kids at school that I was Native American because that is what my grandpa told me. Years later, my aunt, me, and my mom all took 23 and Me and Ancestry.com DNA tests and found out that we don't have a drop of native blood in us, so all these old Native tales my grandpa would tell made me giggle years later. It was all just a lie. There's no bear like Ten Bears.

The Board of Dickheads

The thrift store was a Catholic nonprofit which was run by a board of directors. The board of directors were very rich, preachy assholes. There were two itchy buttholes in particular that stand out in my mind. The first was a man named Jim Cheese. Jim Cheese was an old man with pure white hair. He had a slim frame, and was like a ghost in the way that he would just appear out of nothing. He was truly a child of God.

He would come in and order us around. He would then pat himself on the back for doing God's work. Jim would stop by once a week and cut the lawn for us because he had to show how much humility he had for us poor folk. The store was so cheap when it came to building maintenance. They would either make us do it or this asshole named Harry Peter would do it. If they could have made us do electrical and plumbing work, they would have.

After an employee named Franklin got diagnosed with brain cancer, he became an alcoholic. Eventually Franklin shot himself after a woman coworker moved back to Hawaii. I guess he just couldn't cope. He was so sad this woman moved back to Hawaii that between having a broken heart and cancer, it was just too much to bear.

After his death, Jim Cheese went up to Emily and said, "Yeah, I heard he would fall asleep on the job and was a drinker." Instead of talking about how Franklin persevered through treatments all while still working at the thrift store, good ol' entitled Jim Cheese had to cast a shadow on this poor soul's sad demise. Emily and this scene queen who worked there ended up getting a fish to keep at the register. They named it Franklin.

Harry Peter was an asshole with 2 first names as his alias. With a name like that, no wonder he was such a dick. He must have definitely had a chip on his shoulder after going to school in his formative years. The look of Harry Peter wasn't that interesting; he was a tall man with a solid build. He was years older than my grandpa, and he looked like it. He had peppered hair that he dyed brown sometimes. What was fascinating was his presence. He always had a vibe like he knew something you didn't. He gave off the energy that he knew you were up to something, which gave him a very intimidating demeanor. I could never fully trust him and always felt uneasy around him. Everything he would tell you was cooked up to manipulate you into doing extra work for the peanuts you were paid. Harry Peter's favorite accessory was his holier-than-thou attitude.

Harry Peter had retired from his career as CEO of Master Lock. My friend Nate Schwantz was his neighbor growing up. With Harry Peter and Nate Schwantz both having names that mean phallus, you would think they both resided at 123 Penis Street, Smalltown USA. Sadly, they didn't reside at that address, though.

Nate said that all of Harry Peter's kids hated him because he was a rich, self-righteous prick. We walked on eggshells around him because he questioned us about every little thing that was off about the store. If he treated his kids the way he treated us, it's no wonder they hated him.

To save money, Harry would fix everything himself. The roof leaked, but the thrift store was too cheap to get it fixed. Penny-pinching Harry Peter would show up, get on the roof, and patch it himself. We would later complain to Harry that the roof was still leaking, and he would just hop on the roof again. The roof would continue to leak, so we would collect the water in huge Rubbermaid tubs, which our shoppers would have to swerve around to avoid. We would change the tubs frequently because we had a giant surplus of Rubbermaid tubs. People would donate

Rubbermaid tubs filled with their junk. We would just throw away most of the donations and keep the tub.

The thrift store board members saved up for years to get a new rubber roof. Like the die-hard Christian he was, while the roof was getting replaced, Harry Peter stayed true to the 8th Commandment "*Thou shalt not steal.*" He stole lumber from the roofing company. My grandpa called him out on it.

Peter's reply was, "They're just going to throw this all out anyway."

My grandpa stole a roll of roofing material from the company, too, which made him a hypocrite for calling out Harry Peter. On a sunny day, Harry Peter showed up to check the place out.

He came in and said, "Did someone abandon a car in our parking lot? I see a maroon Toyota Corolla with no windows. Looks deserted."

I was so embarrassed because Harry Peter was talking about my car. I got all red in the face and blurted out, "Ugh, no, Harry. That's my car..."

He chuckled. "Sorry."

Harry was the type of asshole that would point out the obvious to highlight your faults. Not very Christian of him! You would think that a workplace like that would be less judgmental. It hurt me to have someone talk about my car like that, but it came from the asshole Harry Peter himself. If Harry Peter was going to keep showing up unannounced to check the store out, he was going to be a threat to my and my grandpa's side businesses.

Sid was the Board of Dickheads' little toy soldier. He did their dirty work for them. Sid was such a jackass. He was acting like a corporate douche in a religious charity setting.

Sid either didn't understand that something unforeseen could come up or he simply didn't care.

For example, there was a blizzard one morning. My parents and I lived on a lake in Oconomowoc that had only one road in and out. The plows hadn't come through yet. As I left for work in my Toyota Corolla, a box truck got stuck sideways on the entrance side of Elm Street where I lived with my parents. Our neighbors were all lined up in their cars trying to get to work, too. There was a short, chubby truck driver pacing back and forth nervously. I got out to help.

I said, "We need to get this truck moved because I'm late for work!"

The truck driver pleaded with me, "Please help me because if we can't get my truck out, I'm going to be fired. I can't call a tow truck because it'll piss my boss off!"

It was cool because all the neighbors worked together to get the box truck out, so we could get to work. The wheels were spinning in the snow giving the box truck no traction to get out.

I offered, "I'm going home to grab boards. We can put them under the tires for traction."

I got in my car that had snow all over the seat because the windows were stuck in the open position. Snow would just collect in my car, and my butt would be wet every time I drove in the snow or rain. I grabbed the boards and returned to the scene. The tires were still spinning even after we positioned the wood under the wheels. We were close to breaking the truck loose, but no cigar.

Suddenly, a UPS truck showed up. The driver got out with a five-gallon Home Depot bucket full of kitty litter. He dumped the litter under the back wheel.

He said, "I hope this helps. Have a good day!"

The truck got traction in the kitty litter and the driver pulled out. He said, "Thank God! I'm not going to be fired! Thanks, everyone, for all your help!"

I loaded the boards in my car and raced to the thrift store where Sid was waiting for me. I apologized and told him the whole crazy story. He looked at me like the dickhead that he was and said, "Next time, leave earlier! There is no excuse for being late to work!" I remember my jaw dropped. Sid acted like I was a surgeon late for brain surgery but this is just a thrift store that paid their employees peanuts. I thought to myself, "Fuck the thrift store!" It's funny how the Catholic thrift store wouldn't pay me a livable wage, but the Catholic church is the richest entity in the world. While I broke my back for dirt wages supporting the Catholic church, Pope Benedict XVI sat on his gold throne. I felt like the African child sifting through the e-waste landfill looking for cobalt, so Apple can make an iPhone.

I told my grandpa about the UPS driver being so prepared in a time of crisis. My grandpa had worked at UPS, so he giggled because he knew how over-prepared the company is in a snowstorm. He exclaimed, "Buster Brown to the rescue!" Neither Sid nor the board of directors understood it was the little guys who made the thrift store run smoothly.

Wife Swap

You know when two people are fucking each other and it's obvious to everyone? It's almost like they're in heat, and their brains shut off. They're thinking and acting with their genitals. Everyone around them sees it, but they are oblivious to how weird they are acting.

I started to notice Daron going on lunch breaks with Emily. He would follow her around like a puppy. It was very obvious that they were fucking because he wasn't the same donations worker that he had been. He was so far up Emily's ass that it made me want to puke. Daron would wait on her hand and foot when she would do a chore like pricing blankets.

Like clockwork, right about noon, Daron and Emily would go eat lunch at these BMX dirt jumps that were hidden in the nearby Misty Meadows subdivision. I was sure they were fucking, but there was one big problem. Emily was married to this sweet guy who was a middle school teacher. The teacher would bring Emily lunch, and they had a really cute family. They had two boys that they were raising. Emily and her husband had bought a house as an investment property. The teacher used to come in to see Emily on her lunch break, but now the teacher was nowhere to be found. It was all Daron from here on out for Emily.

I was still hanging with Weston and Sarah during this period. They had gotten back together. One weekend, I took them hiking at Nature Hill in Oconomowoc. Nature Hill has trails that loop around or you can head up to the top of this massive hill for a view that is nothing short of breathtaking. The hill overlooks all of Oconomowoc. You can see the quaint downtown area, surrounding lakes, and the abundance of beautiful farm fields. On this day we saw more nature than we were ready for. We got to see human nature. It was the day that I learned how babies are made.

Weston lit a joint and passed it to Sarah. As we approached the side of the hill, we saw at the top a blob of silver blankets that was morphing and shape-shifting. As the joint was passed to me, I saw a human head pop out and the shape of a body riding a naked man. They were fucking! Weston and I gawked as the woman rode him violently in pleasure. I wanted to shout out, "Fuck her harder!" but I held back. Sarah made us leave for another part of the trail and we continued to smoke.

That next Monday, I ran into the sorting room. Emily was sorting through clothes to be priced. I ran in and said, "Oh my god! I saw people fucking at Nature Hill this weekend! They were on the top of the hill going at it!" Emily grinned, but she was red in the face. Years later, Emily's sister Eve would tell me that the people fucking on top of Nature Hill that day were Emily and Daron. My mind was blown, but it all made sense when she spilled the beans to me.

Our responsible manager-type Daron, who preaches peace and love, was committing adultery. Daron wasn't practicing what the thrift store preached with its thought-word-deed ideology. It was like Daron was protesting the Vietnam war while secretly building the bomb! What kind of example was this to the rest of us? That's what I call a positive influence! In the end, I drank the Kool-Aid Daron scooped from the punch bowl. Like Moses did with his followers, I followed Daron into the desert for some years until I finally fucked Eve, Emily's sister, the night manager of the thrift store.

Anyway, Daron and Emily were fucking at this point for sure, and they weren't trying to hide it anymore. There was this alternative scene queen who was a cashier and had become friends with Emily. She had two birds tattooed on her chest. The scene queen wore blue eyeshadow around her eyes, and she dressed like a typical Hot Topic mall rat. She usually had an A.F.I. band shirt on, which was her favorite band. The scene queen had brown hair that had blue highlights in it.

Miss Scene Queen was also friends with Emily's now pissed-off teacher husband. She claimed that Nick (the teacher) caught Daron and Emily making out in Daron's car. It seemed like everyone at work was more interested in how Daron's penis was getting rammed up Emily's vagina than taking in donations or sorting clothes.

A considerable amount of time at the thrift store was spent gossiping about Daron and Emily's sexcapades. I would even gossip with the alternative scene queen girl about it. I could also tell that the scene queen had a crush on Emily's husband. She would go on and on about how Emily was destroying her teacher husband by fucking Daron.

The scene queen claimed to be straight edge, and she dated a guy who was really good at BMX tricks. She seemed like she was happy with the adept BMX guy, but something was about to change. We would spend our breaks at work talking about the latest on Daron and Emily; even though the scene queen was buddy-buddy with Emily herself.

Ultimately, the alternative scene queen cashier got into a fight with Emily about how shitty she was treating her husband. The two of them were in each other's crossfire. The scene queen ended up having a threesome with a friend of hers and Emily's husband! It had become a huge, messy situation. When the teacher graduated high school, the scene queen was just being born. Now he was banging her deep! After a while, the teacher had his fill of revenge on Daron and Emily, but now the scene queen was super pissed at the teacher for supposedly taking advantage of her. Everyone at work couldn't believe what was happening with this bizarre love triangle.

For revenge, the scene queen started fucking Daron, too! She told me! "You will never believe this, but I fucked Daron," was her eloquent confession to me. This alternative scene queen was just really young and horny! Everyone at the thrift store was taking turns on each other. It made me very jealous, to be honest. I started to bully the scene queen when she wanted to fuck my friend from Myspace. It was so shitty of me, looking back. I wish I didn't treat the scene queen like that.

It was all hot until the love triangle turned cold. All of a sudden, Emily was done with Daron's dong. She had decided to get a divorce from the middle school teacher. This was all over the thrift store dirt sheets. Emily and her husband had seemed like the perfect up-and-coming family. Looks are sometimes deceiving, as the portrait of their family faded. Meanwhile, Daron turned into a mopey sad puppy. He still tried to trail behind Emily, but she was over him. She started seeing someone else not long after the dust had settled in the thrift store sex circuit.

The Flat

Now that Emily had ditched Daron, I was becoming fast friends with her. Every Monday at work I would recount my crazy drunken weekend to her. One weekend I got incredibly drunk at my friend Devin's house in Menomonee Falls. Being 40 miles from Oconomowoc, I was too drunk to drive home, so I ended up sleeping in the bushes of someone's backyard until I was sober in the morning. Emily was always telling me to chill out. She loved hearing my stories though. One weekend, Emily invited me out to the eastside of Milwaukee to her brother's house. In attendance was Emily, her sister Eve, Alyssa, the Blanket Girl, and me.

The Blanket Girl was the thrift store employee who priced the quilts and blankets. She was short with light brown hair. She wore glasses which gave her a nerd vibe, but she was anything but a nerd. She loved to smoke marijuana. She also had a steady boyfriend that she loved to cheat on. The Blanket Girl had fucked the whole town, but her boyfriend wasn't aware of the trysts. Alyssa Martin told me that she was at a party where Blanket Girl allegedly took two different guys at two different times into the bathroom to fuck them. Hours later, her boyfriend came to the party to pick her up. Nobody told her man about her extracurricular affairs. Poor guy.

Eve was Emily's sister. She was taller than Emily. Eve had bigger boobs, so she had a thicker frame than her sister. Eve was also extremely beautiful. The sisters got good genes from their parents.

Alyssa Martin gave off the look of "I do drugs." She also gave the vibe of someone who was ghetto. She loved Tupac a lot in middle school. She may have been one of the people who thought Tupac was coming back in the year 2000. Alyssa was a busty gal that was on the taller side. She had a pretty face and dyed her hair blonde.

So, on this day Emily drove us 40 miles east to Wisconsin's biggest city, Milwaukee. Once we got inside her brother's house, I realized that the house was filled with hipster fat cats. I hate to admit this, but I became a bit of a smart-ass when I was in a conversation with some random girl. I told her, "All the best weed comes from Madison, Wisconsin. It gets distributed after that."

She disagreed, "Good weed comes from all over. You're being a know-it-all!"

Years later, I would recall the conversation and realize that I was being a know-it-all. In current times, good weed is everywhere on this planet. Your grandma has bomb weed these days.

Anyway, after I made a fool of myself to that hippie girl, I smoked some weed with the group. Alyssa, Blanket Girl, and Emily were drinking heavily, while I stayed sober. Alyssa was looking really sexy that night; she usually looked ghetto, which was a turn-off. Emily ended up wanting to go home, so we headed towards her car.

We found out that Emily had a flat tire on her car. She turned to me and said, "Travis! Fix this flat tire!"

I shrugged my shoulders and lied: "I don't know how to fix it." Emily ended up calling AAA to put the doughnut on the car, so we could travel home. In the meantime, we took a pic of all the girls and me by the tire throwing up white people gang signs to put on our Myspace pages. A tow truck driver got us back on the road.

Emily dropped us off at the thrift store where our cars were parked. When I got out, I walked Alyssa to Blanket Girl's car and started to make out with her while Blanket Girl got into the car to take them home. I put my hands down Alyssa's pants and started to finger her in the parking lot of the religious thrift store we worked at. She moaned like a dying donkey as I thrust my fingers inside her.

Blanket Girl shouted, "Alyssa, get in the fucking car!"

Alyssa kissed me and said, "I am going to fuck the shit out of you tomorrow! You are all mine!''

I thought, "*Was that a threat?*" I was excited.

The next day, Alyssa was totally indifferent towards me. She seemed more like a friend than a horny monster. I tried to kiss her by the clothes baler during our shift, but she half-assed kissed me. I lost my chance. I should have fucked her there in the confessional at the thrift store parking lot. Father, forgive me.

The Apartment Giveaway

The first time that I met Liam Heineke was in high school, I was introduced to him by an older high schooler named Brett Hawthorne. Brett, Liam, and their friend Maria all sat in the back of my 1994 GMC Jimmy. I blasted Cannibal Corpse's *Butchered at Birth* album and I beat on my rear passenger window until it shattered. I was just beating on the window to the rhythm of the blast beats. It was a total accident that I broke my window. I ended up just taping a black garbage bag to the broken window. I seemed to have a habit of not having windows on my cars even back then! Liam was so terrified that day, but we ended up becoming lifelong friends .... through the trauma of that day.

Years later, Liam would tell me that when he met me, Brett turned to Liam and Maria and said, "You're about to meet Travis and he's crazy."

Brett was right; I am fucking nuts! Fast forward 3 years I was at the store sweeping the aisles with the big broom when I ran into an old friend.

Liam meandered through the aisles of the thrift store. I said, "Hey Liam."

"Hey Travis, I just moved into my first place! What have you all got here?"

With an evil grin, I spat, "Your money's no good here, Liam! Anything in the store is yours if you want it. The thrift store is here to help others, so that is what we will do!"

I justified giving him free furniture because we handed out vouchers to help the poor get furniture. I categorized Liam as poor, so he picked out everything you could imagine for apartment living. He got a standing lamp, couch, chairs, beds, etc.

At one point, he asked, "Can I get this white microwave?"

I shouted, "Fuck yes!"

He was laughing as I gave him a free thrift store shopping spree. He picked everything out and pulled his faded blue 90s pickup truck around to load up his new life.

He shook my hand and said, "I still can't believe you did this for my roommate and me. You gave me an entire house worth of stuff, Travis! You're insane, buddy!"

I was insane to give all that stuff away to my buddy for free, but the truth is that I did it because I believed in him. Part of me had fun showing him my lofty rank at the thrift store. We had just graduated high school, and I was still living at home. It was nice to see a friend taking that first step towards being independent. I would do it all over again. No regrets.

Video Rental

My grandpa and I became our own little mafia around the store. My grandpa always chomped on a cigar while he worked. I was his consigliere. We set up our own side businesses within the confines of the thrift store just like mafiosos would. I was learning from the best! Before my grandma passed, she told me that my grandpa stole from every job that he ever had.

When my grandpa worked for Pabst Brewing Company as a delivery driver, he kept an empty bay in his truck, so he could stash then sell beer under the table to cheap bar owners. When my grandpa worked for Harley-Davidson in their engine department, he would put playing cards in the cyclone fence, go up to the watchtower to see where the blind spot was on the cameras, and then cut a hole in the fence there, where my grandpa knew he could go through unseen. My grandpa then paid his brother to steal motors out of the factory to sell on the black market.

My grandma used to tell me that on top of his stealing, my grandpa would also fake injuries to get worker's compensation. Stealing from our place of employment wasn't new for the "Geier Nation." (This is what we call our family.) Everyone at the store took stuff home without paying for it, but my grandpa and I took it to a whole new level.

We were stealing everything that wasn't nailed down! Sid would order 8 cases of toilet paper. When the shipment of 8 cases of toilet paper would arrive, my grandpa would take 2 boxes for himself. I would usually take one box home to my mom. Sid never noticed that we were also taking home the cleaning supplies.

My grandpa would say, "Beats buying this shit myself."

We built relationships with the regulars and sold them goods out the back door. The first spot I started selling goods to was located two or three doors down from the thrift store. It was a video rental store that bought and sold used video games, consoles, and DVDs. For a span of three and a half years there weren't any video games, consoles, or DVDs being sold at the thrift store because I intervened and sold them to the video rental store three doors down. I got so ballsy that I had a plastic tub hidden behind one of the crappy shelves that our old Board of Dickheads member Harry Peter built.

I would load all the media into that tub and when it filled up, I would haul it into the video store. The owner was this bald, jolly guy who had his several kids putting in shifts at the mom-and-pop Blockbuster. He always asked me where I got the stuff from, and I lied and said that I did cleanouts in Milwaukee.

A couple times I was putting furniture out in the showroom, and I would see the video guy shopping at the store. I would abandon what I was doing and go hide, so he didn't see that I worked there. He would have put two and two together for sure. I always got away before his eyes would catch sight of me.

While I was deep in the video game business, my grandpa was going through all the boxes of jewelry. He got into selling costume jewelry on eBay. He would bring home the stolen goods and have his girlfriend Dorothy post them for sale. He was trying to tap into something that was like my video game business, but he was cashing in on eBay sales. My grandpa started to become jealous of my newfound money-making schemes, but hey! I learned from the best: him.

The Scraps

I was first introduced to the idea of hauling scrap metal from a guy that did scrap metal pickups at our store. He was a fat Hispanic fellow we called Scrap Man Luis. Scrap Man Luis reminded me a lot of the slain singer Selena's father. Luis wore Ray Bans that had a purple tint in the lenses. He had black, greasy hair that was thinning to the point where you could see his scalp. Luis was in his mid-to-late 70s and walked with a limp.

He drove an old white stake bed truck with a dump box. The sides of the box were just old rickety boards. Luis hired bums to help him load and unload the metal.

He would swing by the Salvation Army Homeless Shelter and ask, "Anyone want to make a quick buck?"

On one occasion, the hobo that Luis had hired to haul scrap metal got laid the night before. The hobo's eyes were sparkling more than usual. Luis told us about his "employee's" stroke of luck.

The hobo, in cut-offs, said, "Even the blind find their way to an ear of corn." That statement made me laugh because I had never heard anybody say that before.

Once a week, Luis and the bum would drive to our store to take all of the donated metal that wouldn't make it onto the sales floor. They would load the truck's bed to the brim with scrap metal, and would never put a tarp over the scrap. Luis would drive down the freeway that way, and whatever made it home, made it home.

A volunteer smoking a cigarette watched him pull off with the heaping pile of metal one day on break. She said, "I would hate to be behind that truck on the freeway!"

One time, I asked, "Why do you want all this stuff?"

He gave me some cagey response that let me know to ask a different person. My friend Mike's father was doing community service at the store, so I asked him.

I knew Mike from when we worked together at a Sentry grocery store. We would smoke marijuana in his truck on our break. On one occasion, we smoked Salvia at Arrowhead High School. Mike and I were hallucinating so bad that we were grabbing onto blades of grass because we thought the world had turned upside down. We thought we needed to hang on to Earth for dear life!

Mike's dad was somewhat infamous because of the crime that he committed which resulted in him getting sentenced to perform community service work at the thrift store. Allegedly, he was driving home with his wife when he saw an African American fishing from a bridge in the rural town of North Lake. There was somewhat of an altercation as Mike's dad and his wife drove by. The story that his dad told me was that the victim called his wife a whore. Mike's dad went home, got a gun, and went back to hold the African American at gunpoint while hurling racial slurs at him.

Mike's dad was charged with a hate crime. He ended up spending 30 days in jail and got 200 hours of community service. Half of the community service had to be served at a soup kitchen in the inner city of Milwaukee. He got a light sentence because the victim asked for leniency because he saw a changed man. This all happened during the time Mike and I worked together at Sentry, and I saw what it did to him. Mike was alienated by everyone for the actions of his dad, so I was supportive of Mike. The actions of his dad were not Mike's fault.

I ended up getting fired from Sentry and lost touch with Mike. One day, his dad showed up to do community service at the thrift store. He worked one weekend at the thrift store, and the next weekend at the soup kitchen. Mike's dad was nothing like what the newspaper made him out to be. He was a funny, kind man who made a big mistake. I believe in giving people second chances, so I didn't judge him. It was around this time that I first noticed Luis picking up the scrap metal. I asked Mike's dad why Luis wanted a bunch of junk metal.

He laughed and said, "Luis is making a killing right now. The price of scrap is the highest it's ever been. My buddy manages a transfer site and he makes the workers separate the metal. When he gets a dump truck's worth of pots and pans, he takes them in and makes thousands! You should take the aluminum pots and pans home."

I drove home that day finally knowing what I wanted to do with my life. All my friends moved away to go to college in Milwaukee, and I always felt inadequate because they were navigating college with ease knowing exactly what they wanted to do with their lives. I finally knew that I wanted to be a junk man. My plan was to take my savings, buy a truck, and start hauling scrap.

I parked my Toyota Corolla, with no windows, and I ran inside to tell the good news to my mom and stepdad. My mom wasn't home, and my stepdad was on the couch with his Mac Book out doing his graphic design work. I felt a flutter in my chest like butterflies were flying around inside my body. It felt like I burst in through like the Kool Aid Man was bursting through a wall because of how excited that I was about finally knowing what I wanted to do for a living.

I said to my stepdad, "I know what I am going to be when I grow up! I am going to be a junk man."

He said, "What? What is a junk man?"

I said, "A junk man is a guy who buys a beat-up truck, and hauls scrap metal to get recycled."

My stepdad was uneasy I could tell because all my teenage years I had wanted to be a professional wrestler or a marijuana grower. My stepdad was anal about our lake house, so he didn't like the idea of turning our side yard into an episode of Sanford and Son.

My stepdad snorted like a pig because he was one, and he said, "You're absolutely not doing that here."

My mom came home at that moment too.

I told my mom, "I have finally figured out what I want to be in life, and it's not growing marijuana. I want to be a junk man!"

Every time that I have truly had a great idea that has made me a successful member of society, my mom tells me not to do it. In life, my mom told me not to do junk removal which turned out to buy me a house. She also told me not to be a scare actor in a haunted house which I was a master of horror at. Sadly, my family is afraid of success, so my mom's eyes shot with fear.

My mom said, "In no way, shape or form are you buying a truck to be a junk man!"

We argued the rest of the night about me becoming a junk man, and my parents told me to start small by taking pots and pans home from the thrift store.

I took his advice and I started to take the pots and pans home a little at a time. I turned the loot in and got $400. I was a scrap junkie from there on out. My grandpa was going to help me take all the expensive non-ferrous metal, and I would leave the shit iron for good ol' Luis.

In no time flat, we hid totes behind all the blue laundry carts. We could easily slide the carts in and out to deposit the scrap in our totes. We had a whole scrap stealing system! When a tote would fill up, I would load it into my windowless Corolla. I would then take the scrap home and let it collect in piles. My parents made me keep the scrap under a brown tarp because it was an eyesore. We were stealing all the good scrap and leaving Luis with the low-paying metal. My grandpa and I stored magnets in the donations, so we could test the scrap to see if it contained iron. Luis started to ask us where all of his scrap was going.

My grandpa and I would say, "We're not getting as many donations as we used to."

He knew we were lying through our teeth! He was no longer acting as jolly as he used to. He would just bend over and take it up the ass every week. He would come in and take his laundry bins filled with only sheet iron. If I could have stolen the sheet iron too, I would have. Just being honest: I was money hungry.

I started to make big money selling scrap metal, and that made my grandpa envious! As a result, he started taking all the copper wire off the electronics, knowing that copper was worth good money. My grandpa started to smash the old fat screen televisions to get the copper cone out of it. He had bins and bins of curled-up cords after a while.

I also was making good money from scrapping all of the brass statues that got donated. Again, my grandpa got jealous, so he started saving all the brass statues for himself. My grandpa and I were now in a scrap war. He wanted all the copper and brass which paid the highest. He left me with just the pots and pans. I was the aluminum pot and pan boy! My grandpa was a shithead because that meant that I had to smash all the plastic handles off of the aluminum pots and pans. This was done so the metal recycler would give me a premium price.

I wanted to start my own junk business, so I purchased a big green GMC flatbed truck to start hauling scrap. I was going into business. I never thought I could amount to anything in my life, but now I had finally wanted to do something with my life.

In a weird way, I had finally figured out how to be a bum in life. I wanted to be just like that bum with the cut off shirt that was homeless, but still getting pussy. In my fucked up thought process, I looked up to Luis as a role model. I smiled at Luis as I withheld scrap from him. That's fucked up!

Luis ended up getting so pissed off that I confiscated all the non-ferrous scrap that he told my grandpa, "I have a gun; I will shoot Travis!"

My grandpa laughed and said, "I will shove that gun up your asshole and pull the fucking trigger! Never talk about my grandson like that again."

My grandpa and I just kept on fucking him over until the end of our tenure at the thrift store. In the meantime, I was going to build my new business, The Junk Truck into a recycling force to be reckoned with! This bum was officially in the trash business, and business was picking up!

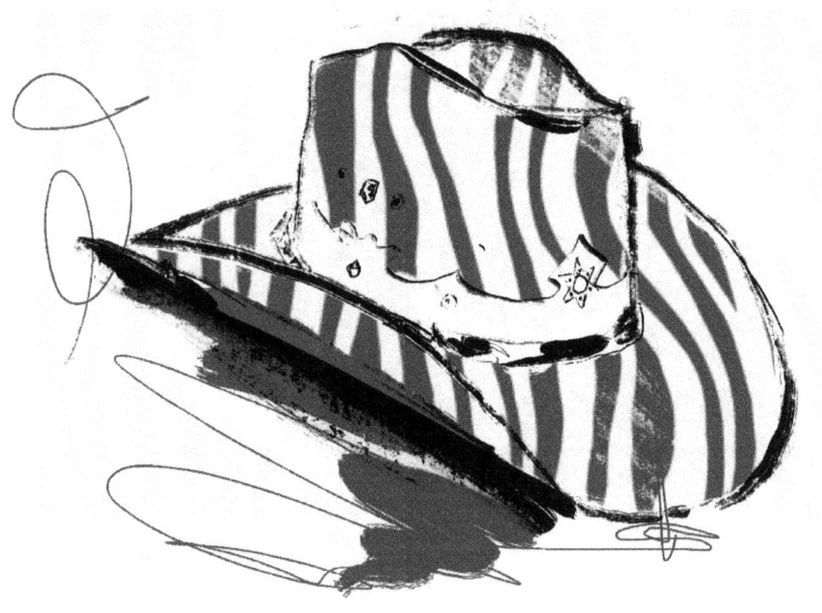

The Zebra Cowboy

One mundane day at the thrift store, Donner and I were just sitting on our butts extremely bored. Donner was pestering me about quitting donations and getting into a union. Donner spoke of the trades as if it was my only choice.

"A boy like you oughta put his card in at the local plumber's union. By the time you're my age, you'll have a great pension to live off of." Donner would ramble on, "A kid your age should get into the heating and air conditioning union!"

I would then respond with something extremely immature like, "I want to fuck my mother!"

As Donner shrugged my lame response off, a car pulled up. The donation consisted of a plethora of old cowboy dress suits. These were high-quality craftsmanship cowboy cloth.

Donner turned to me and said, "You ought to wear one of these suits for your sweetie."

I thought that was a fantastic idea, so I went through all the suits until I found this ugly, cream-colored cowboy suit. When I say "suit", I mean a nice cowboy dress shirt, pants, and boots. The whole nine yards, the suit even came with a cream-colored cowboy hat, but while putting other donations away, I discovered a zebra-print cowboy hat to wear instead for my sweetie.

In my high school years, I had talked a lot with this scene queen on Myspace. After high school, I ended up getting into a serious relationship with her. Her name was Brittany. She stayed in Sussex with her parents, so I reckoned when I wore the cowboy get-up to her house, her parents would probably be there too.

Donner helped me slip into my cowboy attire. He helped me knot my tie like a proud papa would on his son's wedding day. I went into the thrift store bathroom to look at myself in the mirror. I looked fucking ridiculous!

I hopped into my run-down, beat-up Toyota Corolla, and drove 25 minutes in the cowboy get-up. Brittany lived in a wealthy neighborhood because her dad made good money as the CEO of a factory. Whenever my car was there, it probably embarrassed Brittany and her parents, but now even the sight of me was going to really embarrass her.

I stepped out of the car, put my zebra hat on, walked up to the door, and knocked. Brittany answered the door and shut it right away like she'd won the grand prize from Publishers Clearing House. When she opened the door again, her mom was there too and in awe over my Western appearance.

I tipped my hat to her and said, "Howdy, little lady."

Brittany was completely flustered and all red in the face. "I'm going to change into something so we can take a picture together in the backyard." She raced up the stairs to her room.

Brittany came downstairs with a white flower hat on her head and wearing a cute outfit. She went back upstairs to get her tripod and camera. It was a beautiful, sunny day as she set up the camera. She put the camera timer on, then ran back and put her arms around me. I can still see the final picture in my mind. She posted the picture on Facebook and Myspace for everyone to see how foolish her boyfriend was.

We eventually broke up and I didn't talk to her for close to a decade. Ten years after the breakup, I friended her on Facebook. When I looked at her profile, she had shared the picture of us in our cowboy get up with a caption that read, "One of my ex-boyfriends showed up to my house like this. I really dodged a bullet there!" It made me really sad because I always thought that was a fun, spontaneous memory we had together. The zebra cowboy is nothing but a bad memory now.

Donation Landfill

People would donate their garbage to us, and then get offended when we said that the store couldn't use it. My grandpa had a really fast direct approach which he called, "We don't take that shit."

Years later, Daron recalled,

"As we started to get crowded with merchandise on the floor, your grandpa started to get really critical of the donations that would pop up. People would show up with some tattered piece of furniture. We would probably end up throwing the furniture in the compactor. The item would still have some life left if you had to resell it, but he didn't want to take it, so he would just say, "Ahhh, we're not going to take that crap!" The customer would be in shock and say, "Ahhh, you're not going to take my donation? What am I supposed to do with it?" Your grandpa would just mutter, "I don't know. We would just throw it in the dumpster if we accept it here." He'd be real blunt with them. He could have been more tactful about it and kind to the people and say, "Thank you for trying to support our mission, but we can't sell it. We don't have room on the floor. We would have to throw it in the garbage." He went with the direct response. "We're not taking that shit!"

Daron and I talked over one summer as I wrote this book. He had a lot of funny memories of working with my grandpa. Daron also said,

"Your grandpa would curse in front of the customers all the time. I remember trying to let the customers down easy. I'd be like, 'I don't know if they're going to accept this. I don't think we have room on the floor.' I'd do this, so that when your grandpa would talk to them he would just have to say a flat, 'No,' and that would just affirm what I was saying. That way it wouldn't be a punch to their ego. Your grandpa just didn't have a lot of time for people like that! He's dealt with a lot of shitty people throughout his life. I don't blame him for his decision. Working at the thrift store, you should try and maintain a Christian kind of perspective because they're a religious organization. We would laugh about it sometimes."

My grandpa was unholy in the land of the blessed. It was this attitude that started to get the whole small town of Oconomowoc pissed off at us. We became our town's personal dump site. We were getting dumped on by rummage sale leftovers, spring cleanouts, and church donations.

One time, a guy tried to donate a plastic table with 3 legs! My grandpa declared, "We can't take that table because it's missing a leg!"

The guy was offended and replied, "Why not? It's a good table; you can always find another leg!"

Comments like that would drive me insane because it demonstrates that we weren't a thrift store to the public; we were just society's landfill. Another time, someone donated a brand new set of surround-sound speakers still in the box. I was so excited, but lifting them out of the box revealed that every speaker had been punched through. It was like their children popped the speakers, but instead of just throwing it away in their trash can, they took the time to drive it over to dump on us. We ended up having to toss them in *our*garbage.

My grandpa loved grandfather clocks. Unfortunately, not one that came through the donations door was in working order. This impressive grandfather clock was donated by a wife and husband. My grandpa was so excited.

He asked, "Does this clock work?"

The husband smiled and said, "Of course it does!"

The wife nudged him, "Don't lie! You know it doesn't work!"

A customer donated an expensive brand-new blanket. I was going to take it home until I unfolded the blanket. The blanket was covered in dark piss stains. They intentionally folded the blanket in a certain way to hide the piss stains. Why wouldn't you just throw the blanket in the trash? I spent a lot of time throwing away donations that were junk.

A great find for the girls that sorted the clothes was dirty diapers. They would be sorting the bins of clothes and a girl would fish out a poopy diaper. It was probably a mix-up from someone thinking it might be a garbage bag as many of our donations did actually arrive in garbage bags. Blanket Girl and Emily found what they thought was a personal massager that ended up being a dildo.

It was, at times, discouraging. We had to throw away so much shit that we couldn't use. It was starting to look like a dump around the thrift store. Electronics were piled up for weeks; bins of shoes needed to be sorted. We had 17 bins of clothes to sift through. The whole city of Oconomowoc was dumping their rubbish on us, and we just had to take it! My blood was beginning to boil!

My grandpa and I would send people to Lake Country Caring when we couldn't accept the donation. Lake Country Caring is a nonprofit that helps in-need residents of Waukesha County gain access to essential life goods. They are also a donation center.

Lake Country Caring will set you up with basic necessities like clothes and hygiene. People would always complain that they were never open because they were only open 2 days a week. Lake Country Caring was our scapegoat when my grandpa and I didn't feel like accepting donations. We suggested their organization every time we hated our jobs. I use and abuse the thrift store; not the customers!

Repairers Of The Bitch

My grandpa and I were starting to treat the customers like shit. We would reject most of the donations because people would offer up rubbish. My grandpa would flat-out tell people that their donations were crap. I started to get burned out; I was testing my limits with coworkers too.

On top of all this aggression, my grandpa was forcing me to learn how to put the bales on the truck. We would compress old clothes that had rips or armpit stains into bricks. The bricks would weigh 1,000 pounds each, so we would stack them in the back storage area via skid loader. When we had 40 bales and 8 gaylords of shoes, a trucking company from Canada would come out to buy the bales. The company from Canada would recycle our bricks of soiled rags and turn them into J rags. Whatever that is.

The thrift store had a slanted dock, so you had to drive the forklift uphill to get in the tractor-trailer. You would have the forklift slide down the trailer backwards to get out. My grandpa coached me on how to back out of that trailer safely. I approached Emily shaking because I was so scared of running the forks through the side of the trailer.

I was like, "Oh my god, my grandpa is forcing me to do this."

We would only bale bricks of clothes. We never put soiled blankets or winter jackets in the bailer. The thrift store had a relationship with an organization called Repairers of the Breach. They were a homeless rescue mission out of Milwaukee, Wisconsin. Repairers of the Breach would tell us to save textiles like clothes, jackets, and blankets. We would set up a gaylord (a giant box) for them. We would then load the gaylords with jackets or blankets that we wouldn't sell on the racks. This old man in a minivan would come to pick up the items. His van had no seats in the back in order to accommodate the enormous amount of textiles that we would jam-pack in there. I was usually really nice to the guy and would chit-chat with him.

I was annoyed at the sight of him showing up, so I took the pallet jack and started jacking it up violently. To get the gaylord outside by the dumpsters, you had to unlatch this smaller steel door to make it outside with the oversized cardboard box. Instead of doing that I wedged the gaylord between the doors and tried to force the gaylord through in anger. The box was forced through the door. I began loading his car with blankets in a rage. In anger, I mumbled swears under my breath. Once I loaded him to the brim, I didn't say a word. I just took the box and forced the pallet jack back inside.

I look back at my actions as an adult in my mid-30s and I'm honestly embarrassed. I can't count how many people have seen me freak out or have a nervous breakdown. I just try to hold my head high and surround myself with people who don't judge me. That guy was religious, so he gave me a pass. Nah, the guy was probably scared to death of me.

The Truck Drivers

Our sister thrift store in Waukesha had a truck that would do pick-ups. The two truck drivers were friends of mine named Key and Dee. Key was a fat African-American guy. He always wore a brand new snapback hat on his head. He had black curly hair that poked out of his snapback. He was on the shorter side for a man, but not too short.

Dee was a very short, fat Mexican dude. Dee was extremely overweight for being a furniture mover. He had the strangest haircut: the sides were shaved, leaving him with a square patch of hair on top of his head. He slicked back the square patch of hair with some sort of product.

Dee also had facial hair that made him resemble a fat anvil. He always wore a dark blue sweater and black pants that he kept pulling up. Dee walked with a gangster lean . . . mainly due to his weight problem. Key and Dee both lived in the squalid part of Waukesha.

Key and Dee thought I was unhinged because of my antics when they arrived. I would walk into the sorting room and berate a volunteer by asking, "Why were you late this morning?"

Another routine I would do for them is walk into the sorting room and say to the elderly volunteers, "Alright, alright, which one of you has some crack I can smoke?"

Key and Dee would be dying laughing! My masterpiece move was walking up to one of the elderly volunteers and saying, "You need to sign over your social security check to me this month." Sometimes I would even walk into the sorting room, and make a big announcement, "Ladies, I'm going to need you ALL to sign over your social security checks to me this month!" Key and Dee would be cracking up.

Key and Dee would be slacking off sifting through electronics in pursuit of flat-screen televisions to steal. In fact, they stole a bunch of merchandise before the other donation pickups would arrive at the store. Before you knew it, Key and Dee had a little thrift store mafia gig of their own.

Both of the truck drivers had a lot of connections in the Milwaukee area, so they would drive the truck out of Waukesha County to neighboring Milwaukee County and furnish a whole house for cash under the table. They were getting all their relatives to buy furniture from them. Key and Dee would come to work, do donation pickups with the truck, and then turn around and sell the items for cash! There was one big problem though. The side of the donation truck read "The Thrift Store-Waukesha County Pickup." Imagine seeing that driving through the underbelly of the city, the truck was as inconspicuous as a tall tree in the middle of an open prairie. Like my grandpa and I, Key and Dee never got caught with their underground furniture delivery business. They were both kind of shitheads, just like us.

Key was a romantic. He met a girl on Myspace that lived in Michigan. Her name was Espy. Key was living at his mom's house, so he would save every paycheck to make it out to Michigan to see his tootsie. Key became entranced by this woman and we started to not be as close. Every time he would stop into our store, he would always be on the phone talking to Espy.

Ultimately, Key and Dee either got fired or quit. Years later, when I was running my successful Junk Truck business, Key called me and said, "Hey Travis! I'm delivering water for a living now. I don't get paid until next Friday; is there any way you can loan me 20 bucks?"

I agreed to meet him somewhere to loan him the 20. I had my friend Brandon Evans with me who worked at the thrift store, too.

Brandon knew Key, and said, "You know Key is never going to pay you back, right?" I agreed with Brandon as we drove the Junk Truck to the park and ride.

Key spotted my big green Junk Truck with wooden sides right away.

He came up and said, "Thank you, Travis! You will definitely be hearing from me next payday." I rolled my eyes and gave him the 20-dollar bill. I took another look at him, one last time. He patted the hood of his car and shouted, "Thank you, Travis!" I never saw or heard from Key ever again.

The Pimp

Key's counterpart Dee and I were becoming closer friends. Dee had done a stint in prison for stabbing somebody. Thankfully the victim lived, but Dee was not someone to fuck with. Luckily, he thought I was a riot. He loved when I would ask the volunteers for their social security checks or berate them for being late. Dee would also watch me eat whole jars of pickled pepperoncini and jalapenos.

He would always say, "Man, you must have an iron-clad stomach to swallow all that spicy shit."

I was in a committed relationship with Brittany, but I was desperately trying to cheat on her. Dee knew that I was a horndog. He started suggesting that I get a prostitute on the side.

I would say, "I can't do that brother! I would rather cheat on my girlfriend by meeting someone in real life."

Dee would bug me and say,

"Bro, it's like this. If you meet a girl, you have to take her on a date. That costs money, not to mention it takes up your time. Let's say you take a side chick on a date; you'd probably end up spending a hundred bucks to wine and dine her. That's practically the cost of a hooker! You can do the right thing and get a hooker. It will be the same amount as dinner and a movie. The best part is that the hooker will leave the second you are finished with her."

I honestly didn't feel comfortable getting a hooker, but Dee kept insisting. He started inviting me to these prostitute parties at Motel

6 in Brookfield, Wisconsin. Dee lived with a woman who was his meal ticket. Dee only worked part-time, so his girl was paying for everything. She had a kid that Dee was raising also. He would attend these prostitute parties to cheat on his meal ticket.

He filled me in on the details of the parties. Dee said,

"There's a pimp that sets up the party. He charges a door fee to get into the motel room. There are a couple hookers at the party, guys put on rubbers and take turns on these girls."

I felt sick to my stomach hearing this, but I was so horny. I wanted to cheat on my girlfriend so bad that I considered it. For weeks I would turn him down. He kept mentioning that this pimp wanted to talk to me about coming to one of the sex parties.

One day at the thrift store, I got a page over the intercom. "Travis, you have a phone call on line one." I pick up the phone, and what I hear on the other end is the voice of a sleazy African-American. The Pimp called the Catholic thrift store directly to speak with me!

He said, "Yo, bro, we're having a sex party coming up, and I want to see you there!"

My voice was shaking as I was caught off guard. "I will try to make it this weekend," I lied.

The whoremonger said, "Good! Don't bother bringing condoms because I will provide those for you. I hope to see you there, brother!"

I hung up the work line, and without skipping a beat went back to ripping open garbage bags full of clothes and dumping them in the blue laundry bins for sorting.

Stealing Dressers

My grandpa is a master manipulator. He has convinced three different people, in different stages of his life, to sign over the title of their vehicle to him. The first was when my mom was young, and my grandpa spent some time in jail. He convinced another jailbird that he would get him in my grandpa's gang, but first, he had to show his commitment by signing over the keys to his Dodge Challenger. The guy signed over the title to my grandma, and when my grandpa sprung the joint, he was picked up by my grandma in their new Challenger!

The next was after my grandpa divorced my grandma, he let a biker stay with him. The guy was an awesome concrete finisher. The only problem was that my grandpa's new roommate thought he was going to marry an exotic dancer. He left his job and waited for a stripper to show up at a hotel for three days. The guy was down on his luck, so my grandpa took advantage of him. The guy had a very expensive Harley Davidson Shovelhead, but he needed a car. This was the perfect opportunity to get the roommate's motorcycle into his greedy hands, so my grandpa traded his Cadillac for the Harley-Davidson Shovelhead. The roommates' sisters were mad at my grandpa because the Cadillac was worth far less than the sought-after Harley. Reluctantly, the sisters brought over the title to the bike. My grandpa sealed the deal on the trade and then locked the guy out of the house.

The roommate called my grandpa from a few miles down the road and said, "Hey! The windows already stopped working on the car you traded me, fucker!"

Years later, my grandpa stole a vehicle out from under someone and this time I actually supported the thievery. My grandpa was in A.R.M., which stands for Alcohol Recovery Motorcycle Group. He was sponsoring one of the members of the club. One day he got a call from his sponsee. The guy informed him that he had been charged with sexual assault of a child. My grandpa would never help a child molester, so he helped himself to the baby fucker's stuff.

Right away he told the guy, "We need to get all your vehicles out of your name because the courts are going to seize everything." The child molester ended up signing the title of his truck over to my grandpa. My grandpa cleaned the guy out of all his power tools. The baby fucker was a commercial painter, so he had all these expensive air compressors and gadgets for painting that my grandpa saw as free money. This is proof that my grandpa is a master manipulator. This may not be his last foray into tricking someone out of a vehicle. He will take advantage of anyone.

The true victim of his lies and manipulation was the thrift store. He would especially take advantage of the manager Sid. Sid's remarkable foolishness was too big a temptation. My grandpa had a new side hustle at the thrift store which brought his manipulative skills to new heights. He was always looking to make a buck and could smell quick money. He soon turned an idea he saw on the show Antiques Roadshow into cash. He would steal valuable antique furniture that was donated and take it to an auction house to sell for his own profit.

At his home, he had a whole barn filled with antiques that never made it to the thrift store floor. A pair of dressers from the early 1900s came in. My grandpa had his white Toyota Tundra parked in the space next to the donation door.

We loaded the dressers onto the bed of his pickup right as Sid came storming out in a huff, "Did you pay for these dressers?"

My grandpa, still on the truck, jumped off and lied right to Sid's face, "Of course I did!"

My grandpa concluded his lie by walking away from Sid after that exchange. Sid, again, was so dumb and lazy that he just took my grandpa's word for it. Sid didn't even go up to a cashier that day to ask about if my grandpa had actually paid for those dressers. The stolen furniture nested in my grandpa's truck for the rest of his shift that day. At 5:00, my grandpa rode off into the sunset with his stolen goods.

My grandpa had Sid under hypnosis during our work shifts. Sid was entranced with my grandpa and held him in high esteem. They even went to a Milwaukee Brewers game together once. When the Brewers scored, Sid jumped up as if he wanted my grandpa to high-five him with both hands.

My grandpa looked with disgust at Sid and said, "What are you? Ten years old? I'm not doing that!"

My grandpa still had to act too cool for Sid because he had to give off that badass biker vibe. He had to be in control at all times. He really was a wolf in sheep's clothing.

100
100
100
100
100

Safe Crackers

Sid loved to hire young girls because he was a creepy old man who liked to gander at young, hot trim. His standard operating procedure was as follows:

Step 1: hire cute girls.

Step 2: give them a key to the store.

It seemed like the whole town had a spare key to the thrift store because Sid would hand them out to the young lasses like they were trick-or-treat candy. He never had the notion to get the key back after they were fired or quit.

An old acquaintance of mine that I went to school with got hired at the thrift store a while back. She was a thick girl with giant tits, so Sid was drooling over her right away. Her name was Alyssa. She had Sid wrapped around her finger like he was her sugar daddy. Kind of like how I had her wrapped around my finger in the parking lot.

Alyssa was trouble for sure. When she was 13, she stole a car that was running. The guy was warming up his car in the dead of winter, and Alyssa just hopped in and took off with the car. It ended up being Daron's friend's car and she led them on a high-speed chase. Daron chased her all night until she crashed his friend's car in a field. She was arrested. Years later, Daron would put two and two together about who he was working with.

Alyssa was a good thrift store worker, but she ran with a rough crowd. She would check every pants pocket and would sometimes pull out 20, 40, or 60 dollars. Sid wanted to fuck her so bad that he forced Emily to train Alyssa how to be the night manager. That was until the day all the employees were informed that Alyssa jumped out of a moving car when she was blackout drunk. She was having a panic attack about her dead father, so she bailed at high speed. She broke her leg so badly that she had to always be lying down. This concluded her employment at the thrift store. We needed a few new cashiers to take her place, so we hired my mom's crazy friend Shelly, and one of Daron's friends, Sadie Mueller.

Sadie Mueller was a middle-aged woman who had adult acne. She had long, light brown hair. Sadie was tiny in stature, which made her look like a little doll. She looked like she had done a lot of drugs which was very true.

Crazy Shelly looked like a 1980's video vixen who ate too much McDonald's. She was still pretty, but she was in her late 30s or early 40s. She was a brunette with an '80s teased hairstyle.

My mom bumped into Crazy Shelly in town while she was living in her car. Before the thrift store, Crazy Shelly worked at McDonald's in Oconomowoc. She told us she quit because some idiot was mopping with ice-cold water!

She told us, "I knew McDonald's was below me when I saw him using cold water to mop the red tile in the McDonald's kitchen."

Crazy Shelly landed in legal trouble by driving southbound in the northbound lane going 70 mph on the interstate, what the police call a "wrong-way driver." When she got out of the car after pulling over, she had no pants or underwear on. She was just in a t-shirt and claimed to be going out for a pack of smokes. Shelly was definitely starting over in life. That's when my mom convinced my grandpa to let Crazy Shelly rent a room at his house.

Sid only hired Crazy Shelly because he had the hots for my mom. Sid saw it as doing my mom a favor to get in her good graces to hopefully fuck her. Shelly was down on her luck, so my grandpa let Crazy Shelly live with him in a spare room. She was going to 12-step meetings. Previously, Shelly lived in LA, worked for Mark Burnett, and was in recovery.

Before Crazy Shelly moved in with my grandpa, she stayed two nights over at Sid's house. I had scored her an interview with Sid and he offered her a place to stay. She swears that he was upstairs, and she turned on his television. It was a rear projection television. The second the screen had a picture it was hardcore gay porn.

She told my grandpa, "Sid is a Jeffrey Dahmer-type psycho."

Once Crazy Shelly was living at my grandpa's house, he was working the 12 steps with her. His favorite step in recovery was the 13th step. The 13th Step is a joke in Alcoholics Anonymous about when someone in recovery has sexual relations with a newcomer to the program.

My grandpa would brag to me, "Travis! Crazy Shelly is giving me tune-ups regularly."

I told my mom and she was disgusted, but at least Shelly was working and had a roof over her head. One night, Sadie and Crazy Shelly closed the store. They counted the money and closed down the drawers. They both signed off on the receipt that showed the day's financials.

That Monday, I walked into a dark store. Detectives and police were questioning employees.

I looked at Daron and said, "Did the store get robbed?"

Daron looked somber; he turned to me and said, "Yes, someone cleaned out the safe."

Gossip spread like a California wildfire; everyone had their own theory as to who the robbers were. My mom's friend Shelly and

Daron's friend Sadie were instantly terminated. Emily and Daron were the ones who opened the safe that fateful Monday morning, so naturally the police were grilling them.

All Emily remembered was that she was still half asleep, so when she opened the safe and saw nothing was in it she did a double take. They asked Emily if she would submit to a lie detector test. She was also being questioned by police about her sexual relationship with Daron and the status of her marriage.

The police grilled my grandpa about his possible involvement, but he ended up throwing Daron under the bus. My grandpa ended up giving Daron the cold shoulder for a couple of weeks because he thought Daron and Emily were in on it.

All the employees were divided as to which woman took the money. I clearly remember fighting with Daron by the baler about which girl took the money from the safe.

I shouted at Daron, "My mom said Shelly is crazy, but she isn't a thief!"

Daron sternly replied, "I've known Sadie since high school, and she wouldn't steal the money, so it has to be Shelly!"

Shelly was still renting a room at my grandpa's house and she didn't come home the night of the robbery, so the cops and my grandpa thought that she did it. The sad part was when Shelly got axed from her employment, my grandpa caught her stealing his girlfriend Dorothy's pain meds. Now she was without a job and without a home. Shelly got kicked out onto the street with her black garbage bags.

Detectives were on the case, but they didn't know what to think. A safe opened and closed seemingly by magic. There were no cameras in the store, and there weren't any unusual fingerprints on the safe. They must have worn gloves. It wasn't like the safe was broken into.

The girl who priced the blankets told me, "You know, Alyssa is hanging out with some crackheads right now and she has a key. Alyssa or one of her accomplices posted on Facebook bragging about robbing the store." The Blanket Girl saw the post and called the detectives.

The police didn't know how to use social media at the time, so they didn't follow up on the lead for over a week. The Oconomowoc Police actually had to sit down with the girl who folded the blankets and have her show them where on the Facebook wall to find the post. They pinned the robbery on Alyssa and her merry band of crackheads. She gave the key to these very bad guys and they just opened the door, went to the safe, and loaded up all the money. They even locked the safe and locked the door for us! All because Sid never asked for the key back.

It just goes to show you how Barney-Fife-foolish our Oconomowoc small-town cops were. They were accusing people of affairs and pointing fingers at people down on their luck. It was the early days of Facebook, so the pigs weren't checking social media to crack the case.

Years later, Emily told me that Sid convinced the cops that Crazy Shelly was to blame for stealing the money out of the safe, so that is why they started spinning wild tales. In reality, Sid was the crazy one. By Sid handing keys out like candy, the keys got into the wrong hands. Just goes to show, Cabbage Patch kids should not be in positions of trust.

The Bobblehead Guy

When I was a kid, I lived in an apartment in Oconomowoc, Wisconsin. It was low-income housing for single mothers and their children. There was a maintenance guy named Gordy who was the stereotypical maintenance dude. He was old, fat, and wore a button-up shirt that exposed the gray follicles of his hairy chest. He always smelled of booze. He was a grumpy bastard, but he had his place.

When I was a kid, I sometimes would have an insane temper tantrum where I would slam the door. I slammed the door so hard that the door handle put a huge hole in the wall. The apartment managers inspected the apartments once a year, and our inspection was coming up. My mom wanted to hide the hole in the wall, so she had me draw a picture of my mom and I by a rainbow. She placed my masterpiece over the hole, but when Gordy came, he made sure to feel the drawing for a hole.

He turned to my mom and said, "You're busted."

I still laugh that my mom would think that a crude kid drawing directly in the line of fire of the door handle would throw them off my trail of destruction.

The apartment corporation felt bad for Gordy because he was a stone-cold alcoholic. Eventually, just like one-armed Buck, he got canned for his alcoholism. The new maintenance guy was a dick and was on top of things. Unlike Gordy, he was a by-the-book kind of guy when it came to the upkeep of the Jeffworth Apartments. I hated the new guy and wanted the gutter drunk Gordy back. The new guy was very stern, which I wasn't used to as a child of a single mother.

Gordy has to be dead by now, but his successor showed up at the thrift store one day. He was old at this point, and seemed fake-jolly. He was close to retiring from Jeffworth Apartments. We chatted about his time there, but he didn't remember me at all. That was probably a good thing because I was a little shit growing up.

The maintenance guy I feared as a kid asked me, "Got any bobbleheads? I'll give you a couple bucks for them."

I dug on the shelves and gave him some bobbleheads that had been collecting dust. He gave me a couple bucks, and I pocketed the cash. Every week, he would pop in and inquire about bobbleheads. My grandpa was sure that the guy resold them for way more than he was giving me, but I didn't care because he was always greasing my palm. I sold him bobbleheads until I left the store. It was so weird to be helping out the maintenance guy who put the fear of God into me as a child.

Bicycles

My grandpa started to get annoyed by the regulars who would come in, buy something, and resell it on eBay. There was this older couple that came in every day that my grandpa disliked from the start. The guy would not leave him alone about buying bicycles for cheap; he was relentless. My grandpa gave in to selling bikes to the guy for about $20 a bicycle. My grandpa would set them aside in the donation center for the elderly couple. They would pull up with their immaculate Mercedes Benz with their tacky dyed light brown hair to collect the bicycles.

It turned out that the guy who bought bikes from my grandpa had hundreds of bikes under tarps in his backyard in Merton, Wisconsin. He would seek out bicycles at rummage sales, thrift stores, and online. Once he got the bikes home, he would fix them and sell them. The town of Merton was after him about the bikes under the tarps. Neighbors were complaining the bicycles were an eyesore. Eventually, he opened a bike shop inside an auto body shop. The problem was that he wanted an arm and leg for each used bike. He was paying a measly $20 for the bikes we stole for him at the thrift store; he should have given people a better deal.

The bike couple would kiss our asses to get their greedy hands on the bicycles for cheap, and my grandpa was eager to take the money. The bicycle guy's wife made us bran muffins once. I was gaining a lot of weight from eating at Kwik Trip every day, so I really didn't need to be tempted with muffins. My grandpa was off the day she brought the muffins in. She had a big glob of butter for us to spread on the delicious muffins. I ended up eating all four of them. I tried to save two muffins for my grandpa, but my lack of willpower towards food wouldn't allow that. The next day when the couple asked my grandpa how the muffins were, it was revealed that I was a fat ass for eating all the muffins myself.

My grandpa was very pleased with himself whenever he sold a bicycle to the elderly couple. He loved to find new schemes to put into motion at the thrift store. He was letting his newfound power and greed go to his head. Now, my grandpa and I would stop at nothing to sell the entire store.

Preachers

One afternoon, two elderly African American gentlemen showed up at the thrift store. They approached my grandpa while he was pricing furniture. The aged men introduced themselves: "We are preachers that are looking to help our congregation out by looking for appliances for the needy. We work for God, sir!" The preacher duo were looking for a washer and a dryer. My grandpa took them to our appliance area. The thrift store sold appliances, but they never tested them before letting customers lug them home. Customers would be pissed when they paid for a fridge, took it home, hauled it down to the basement, and then found out it was a dead appliance.

After the customer would haul the junk appliance down to their basement, they would then have to haul it back upstairs, load it back in a truck, and return it. The customers would always return the dead appliance in an evil mood because of this. My grandpa would tell Sid to stop accepting appliances, but it fell on deaf ears.

Anyway, my grandpa loaded the preachers up with the appliances. He pocketed their money, and the two preachers vanished. They returned with an empty truck after heading back from unloading the washer and dryer. The preachers asked my grandpa, "Do you have anything else that we could work out a deal on?" With the potential of free money in his very near future my grandpa led them into the warehouse.

With their truck parked by the dumpsters, the duo came inside the warehouse and evidently noticed the pile of electronics collecting dust. The thrift store only let volunteers go through the electronics. The electronics guys were all old geezers that only volunteered once a week. This caused the electronics to pile up.

The one electronics guy was an old retired electrician named Abe. He banked at my girlfriend Brittany's sister's work. Brittany's sister was a teller at the bank. One day Abe from electronics mentioned to Brittany's sister that he volunteered in electronics at the thrift store.

She said, "My sister's boyfriend and his grandpa work there! His name is Travis!"

Abe looked at her and politely said, "Travis and his grandpa are characters."

We were certainly being characters with these preachers by letting them in the warehouse to case the place.

One preacher asked, "How much for all those stereos?"

My grandpa came up with a cash price for the preachers, as they broke the first commandment by participating in this black market electronics deal. They loaded up their truck with stereos until it was completely packed. They asked my grandpa about a thrift store in Hartford, Wisconsin.

My grandpa replied, "Fuck no! You are two black guys with a truck full of electronics in the small town of Oconomowoc. You need to get on Highway 16 and get your asses back to Milwaukee. Also, you two get pulled over . . . you don't know me!"

Oconomowoc was a very small town in the mid-2000s. It was almost 99 percent Caucasian. The town had one of everything when it came to being culture-friendly. There was one Black family, one Asian family [who ran the Chinese restaurant], one Mexican family, one gay guy, and so on. With there only being one Black family in the whole town, the preachers of God and their shabby truck stuck out like a sore thumb. Oconomowoc tends to be white-centric, so it was a good move for them to skip town before a redneck cop profiled them. They got in their beater truck and suddenly they were gone, never to be seen again!

Cigarettes

Ever since I can remember, my grandpa has always had a cigar hanging out of his mouth. You could even catch a glimpse of him on the freeway with a cigar in his mouth as he passes you at 70 mph on his Harley full dresser. My grandpa smoked 100 fat cigars a week when he was a semi-truck driver for the UPS truck division. Old habits die hard. My grandpa had a cigar in his mouth every moment of the workday at the thrift store. If he was on the showroom floor pricing couches, he had a lit cigar in his mouth. If he was taking in a donation from a patron's car, he had a cigar hanging from his mouth. Customers would complain about him smoking in the store, but my grandpa didn't give a fuck. At his age, he was out of them.

His thoughtless habit started to rub off on me and I got careless about smoking while taking in donations. One time, I reached into a patron's car with a cig in my hand to fetch the donation and there was a baby sitting in a car seat inside the car. The customer lost their shit and complained to Sid about it. Sid yelled at me . . . even though he smoked in the donation room, too. Sid would sit in with all the new female hires, smoking away.

Sid loved to hire women as cashiers, and men as donations attendants. He wanted the girls close to him. Sid hired this late 20s redneck girl. She smoked a lot of cigarettes out back by the dumpster when there weren't any customers in the store. One day, she broke Sid's heart and announced that she was pregnant. An odd thing happened; the pregnant girl kept taking cig breaks! As the months went on, she started to show. She was a vision with a protruding baby bump and a cig hanging from her mouth. I would be out there just chatting with her while she harmed her fetus.

I chose to mind my own business by not admonishing her about it. I hope that the baby came out healthy. That pregnant girl wasn't the only one infecting the youth with tobacco.

The thrift store had an arrangement with the Lake Country court and school systems. You could perform community service because of a sentence by a judge or because your school mandated you. You could also volunteer out of the goodness of your heart if you so desired. The nearby military academy bussed a group of their students here to do just that.

The military academy is a prestigious, upscale school where rich parents dumped their kids they didn't have time for. Most of the kids that came to work on Saturday at the thrift store were white affluent snobs from Illinois. The kids were bussed in on a black bus and they wore black and white tracksuits.

The kids refused to do any work; they would just fool around slapping each other in the nuts while pointing and laughing. They spoke Spanish to each other on purpose because I didn't know how to speak it. They were required to learn Spanish as part of their curriculum, but they used it to talk shit about me. They goofed off in front of customers and demanded that I buy them cigarettes. A pack of cigarettes in Wisconsin in 2008 possibly cost $3.75. At the military school, cigs or chew would sell for $30 a pop. The military academy had a black market, similar to how prisons have a smuggle ring.

There was this older kid from Seattle. Everything out of this kid's mouth was a lie. He claimed that his neighbor was the guitarist of the band called This Providence. I don't know if that was a lie or not because why would you lie about a tiny band that had modest success?

The kid said, "My neighbor quit This Providence to become a barber because music was too hard to make a living at."

Anyway, this kid always had $500 or $600 in cash on him. He would write out a list of tobacco products that he wanted. I would go across the street and hand the same list to the girl at Kwik Trip; I would come back with an amount of cigarettes that would supply the entire U.S. Army.

On one occasion, the clerk at Kwik Trip questioned me and said, "Are you sure that all this tobacco is for you?"

I gulped and replied, "Of course."

You're probably wondering why I would do this. The answer is that I really don't know. I probably felt bad for them because they were all very troubled. Their parents didn't care about them at all, so I gave in to their demands. After they would have their surplus of cigarettes, they would smoke them by the compactors.

One kid was 11 years old; he would be out by the dumpster taking a cig break.

I said, "You're way too young to be a smoker."

He yelled back, "Shut the fuck up, bitch! Don't tell me what to do. You're not my parents!"

That 11-year-old had a bad potty mouth. All the military kids did was slack off and smoke cigs, so my grandpa eventually told their coordinator at the academy not to bring them anymore. Just think, today that potty-mouthed, nicotine-addicted boy might be commanding an army somewhere.

Knight In Shining Armor

Sid had a friend named Chaz who he offered a job; Chaz was going to work in donations with us. My grandpa and I were concerned because we didn't need him telling Sid about us stealing. We had to agree to this Chaz character working alongside us.

Chaz's first day had us relieved. Chaz was a funny guy; it seemed like he didn't like Sid either! Chaz looked like he just stepped out of a time machine from 1984. He wore acid-washed jeans with an oversized sweater that said, "B.U.M. Equipment." To top it off, he wore a thick gold chain, like his nana gave it to him. Chaz was a short guy. His hair was dyed blonde, but it was so badly dyed that it was orange. He wore tight jeans, like he was about to head to the Whiskey a Go-Go to see Motley Crue. His skin was made of red leather from tanning too much and choking down cigarettes. He was always munching on Mike and Ike's candy. Chaz made us laugh because he would come in from hard lines with something ceramic and fragile.

He would say, "Do you know what this is, Travis? Do you know how much this heirloom is worth?"

He would instantly drop the item on the ground like it was an accident and would watch it shatter into a million pieces.

"Oh my god! NOOOO!" It would really lighten up the mood on a bad day.

When Chaz spoke, he only talked about three things: '80's hair metal music, cocaine, and injecting anabolic steroids. He grew up in Rockford, Illinois in the 1980s. He loved talking about the glory days of 1980's hair metal excess. Chaz talked about cocaine like it was his kid and he was proud of it. At first, Chaz was kind of out of shape, but during his tenure at the thrift store, he started doing steroids. He would always talk about Tiger Blood, which was an underground form of testosterone. Chaz lived in his parents' basement in Watertown, Wisconsin.

He bragged that he used to do coke and take a nap afterwards. He secretly bought cocaine at the thrift store from a volunteer who was doing community service. The kid who sold the coke said Chaz was in a sad mood when he made a purchase. It was because he couldn't stop doing coke as a result of his addiction and sadly he knew it.

He met and started dating an older woman with an '80's rock-era video vixen haircut. The relationship turned serious and Chaz was smitten. Chaz's only friends were Sid the store manager and me. He asked us if we would help him propose to his girlfriend. He had a looney proposal idea that I'm glad I got to be a part of.

His idea was to dress up as a knight, ride in on a horse, and propose to his girlfriend, who would be sitting on a throne. I honestly didn't think he could pull this off, but he kept insisting on practicing at Sid's house. In his backyard, Chaz gifted us two knight costumes from Spirit Halloween. We practiced our routine of guiding him on the horse, etc. Chaz was spending thousands of dollars to make this knight in shining armor proposal happen, so it was a good thing that he was saving money by living in his parents' basement.

As the week of the proposal approached, Chaz was pulling out all the stops. He was going to lie to her and tell her that he ordered a limo for her to go to work at the hair salon she worked at. There was a Ponderosa Steakhouse next to the hair salon. Chaz worked it out with all the businesses, so they were aware of the insane proposal stunt Chaz would be pulling off.

Chaz was worried that I would not show, but I was eager to watch this play out. I showed up that Saturday morning before my call time. A little while later, a truck with a horse trailer pulled up in the Ponderosa Steakhouse lot. I dressed in my Spirit Halloween knight costume while Chaz suited up in a real suit of armor. Chaz started to get on the horse and practice coming from around the building. He'd set up a real high-quality throne in the hair salon parking lot. Chaz rode over to the building we would hide behind with the horse. Chaz had handed me a really expensive sword with a love letter to her engraved on it.

As showtime drew near, a crowd started to gather to see what the big fuss was. At 9:00 AM, a limo pulled up, and his sweetie was directed to sit on the throne and was handed a dozen roses. We were hiding behind a strip mall until the song started. Over the PA system, the song, "It's The Final Countdown" started playing and a shot of fog spurted out from a fog machine. Sid and I walked next to Chaz on the horse in his real shining armor. As the 80s hit played, people watched with smiles on their faces. Suddenly, the song stopped, and was replaced with the powerful love ballad, "(Everything I Do) I Do It For You" by '80's Canadian rock sensation Bryan Adams.

Chaz got off his horse and I knelt down (this was rehearsed) and I presented him with the real sword with the love letter engraved on it. I was interested to see what his girlfriend thought, so I looked over at her. She was clutching the roses and in hysterical tears. I will never forget the memory of her sobbing for joy while that cheesy Bryan Adams song played.

She was eating it up! He then got down on one knee and gave her his sword and slipped a ring on her finger. Chaz had invited the press to come. The Watertown Daily Times printed a photo on the front page of the next Monday's newspaper. It was a picture of Chaz on the horse and me staring up at him. It was a memory I will never forget, and I still cherish to this day. Sadly, after the elaborate proposal that cost thousands, Chaz's fiancée ended up calling off the wedding. Sometimes you aren't looking for your knight in shining armor after all.

Tap Out

During this time, the thrift store sent us to forklift school. We had been operating the forklift at the thrift store without a forklift certification. Harry Peter wanted us to get certified because they feared OSHA would find out that we were operating forklifts without a license.

The class of thrifters was going to be Daron, my grandpa, and I. It was funny to drive with the three of us in my grandpa's truck. We headed to Pewaukee to attend the college course. We spent half the day in a class, took a test, and went out to the warehouse at the Waukesha County Technical College to play on a real forklift. The instructor told us to grab the pallet with the gaylord off the top shelf, but not to be slick and lower the mast while we grabbed it. All 3 of us were slick and lowered the mast as we pulled the box off of the shelf. I remember that I was kind of nervous as I grabbed the box off of the shelf, took it around the building, and put it back up on the shelf. We all left that day with laminated cards that said we were forklift certified. The next morning, we were all ready to be legal eagles on the forklift. We were ready to make OSHA proud.

That day, my grandpa had Daron standing on the top stack of the 40 bricks of clothes. We needed to get the last 1,000-pound brick on the stack.

Years later Daron would tell me, "Oh man, I was hoping I didn't piss him off. He could just leave me here to die!"

Later on, the donations slowed down for the day. The volunteers were politely pricing clothes and shoes. It was back to business as usual, but not for my grandpa and I. We were up to no good. Tensions were high between us. My grandpa was resentful of how many donated items I was turning into stone cold cash.

My grandpa and I were stealing so much stuff from the store and selling it. We became competitive and that led to us stepping on each other's toes a bit. My grandpa got greedy and started to want a cut of my scrap side business and the video game heist. He was acting like he was Tony Soprano. Here's how that played out: we were working a shift that was slow. My grandpa had a cigar in his mouth, and he was saying some crazy shit that made no sense. I don't exactly remember the dialogue, but it was my grandpa strong-arming me into letting him in on one of my thrift store hustles.

His psychotic, ass-backwards statement made me say, "Fuck that!"

I then turned around and went through the circle window grocery doors. I was walking in the sorting room past a large number of elderly volunteers.

An enraged scream of, "HEY! GET BACK HERE!" rang out in the sorting room.

I started to run away because I knew the devil was coming. I made it to the baler and started using the machine.

My grandpa caught up to me and began choking me violently while screaming in my face. He did that thing where you choke someone and shake them at the same time.

He got in my fucking face and screamed, "DON'T YOU EVER FUCKING TURN YOUR BACK ON ME EVER AGAIN!"

He let my neck go and walked off back through the sorting room. Somehow no volunteer ever complained about that incident. It might have been that they were afraid of Tony Soprano, too.

I was not scared by the attack; I just shook it off. Years later, I told that story in one of my improv practices and my entire comedy troupe was horrified. They all stood and listened in silence.

One member said, "Travis, that is sad because that is abuse."

I never really thought about it that way...

If I told my grandpa that it was abuse, he would have said, "What? No, don't make me slap you!"

It's just laughed off, which makes me giggle at how insane he really is.

A Fecal Matter

The thrift store usually didn't give people a full forty hours a week to work. To get my forty hours, I would have to come in an hour early every day to clean the bathrooms. The bathrooms at the thrift store looked like the grimy bathroom from the first *Saw* film. It was something out of a horror movie.

Sid's favorite move was to call me over the intercom when someone had a bad accident in the shitter. It was like he got off on knowing that I was the turd boy who had to deal with the bathrooms. As if I wasn't down in the dumps enough already.

He would say over the loudspeaker, "Travis, report to the women's bathroom." I could practically see his sneer.

He wanted the whole store to know that I was a piece of shit. On top of that, people were disgusting pigs when it came to shitting out their asses. Which gender do you think had the most gruesome shitter? The answer is women. They had the most disgusting bathrooms. They would leave bloody tampons on the floor! A few times I would go into a woman's bathroom stall and there would be period blood smeared all over the walls. That shit was extremely tribal if you ask me. The bloody tampon would be laying on the floor with menstrual hieroglyphics written on the stall wall in some foreign language from days gone by.

Men are truly from Mars and women are from Venus. The girls would fill the feminine product waste basket with shit-stained toilet paper. Women would drop the biggest plops in the toilet too. If there was an accident in the women's bathroom it would always exclusively be diarrhea. Every fucking time. The toilet would be plugged up. Women had the nastiest diarrhea compared to the men, but a male beat them one time in the battle of the bathroom stall disasters.

The store was open with a few customers walking the aisles. I just had a big rush of donations come in. I needed to take a piddle, so I entered the men's bathroom. The bathroom had one urinal with a smaller toilet stall. Next to that was a handicapped stall. I took my piss, and I started walking out without washing my hands because I'm disgusting. I could sense that I wasn't alone so I needed to get the fuck out of there.

A worried voice rang out, "Please help me! Don't leave me here!"

I rolled my eyes and muttered, "Fuck" under my breath. I walked up to the stall and knocked.

The person said, "HELP! I'm in a wheelchair and I've fallen off the toilet!"

"Are you decent?"

"I will try to pull my pants up, yes!"

I walked in and saw a wheelchair in the corner, a toilet clogged with diarrhea, and a man had fallen off the toilet. I stood there and pulled him up to jimmy him on the edge of the toilet bowl. Next, I got him back on the toilet to wipe his ass. He thanked me as I held my breath from the poop particles in the air.

I looked back at the toilet and there was a ridiculous amount of toilet paper clogging the bowl with light brown turds floating around. The poop looked like wood pellets for a Traeger grill. After he wiped his ass, I pulled up his pants and got him back on his wheelchair as I went blue from holding my breath. It was really gross, but very gratifying to help someone in need. I do not know what physically disabled people go through, so it was a blessing to be there in his time of need. I briskly walked out of the bathroom, still without washing my hands. Glad to do my job! Bathroom detail!

Sundae Funday

Eve was the nighttime manager at the thrift store. She got paid $8.50 an hour to close the store at night. A plethora of customers would call and ask to speak to the manager. Eve would kindly answer their questions.

On one shift, she was sorting the shoes when over the intercom a voice said, "Eve, line one."

I raced Eve to the phone and won.

I answered the phone in a female voice, "Hello."

I pretended to be a female with a high-pitched voice. The woman at the other end of the line asked some questions. I responded; meanwhile, Eve was frantic.

She was full of angst, mouthing the words, "What are you doing?"

I shook her off and then I admitted to the caller that I wasn't a woman.

I said, "I'm sorry. I'm just joking, I'm not Eve. This is Travis in donations."

The woman was disgusted and said, "What you just did was very unprofessional. I won't be shopping there ever again!"

Eve was so pissed. She said, "You just made us look like fools. Why would you pretend to be me?"

I said, "It's fine! Come here and watch something with me, Eve."

Everyone remembers the viral shit porn, *Two Girls One Cup*. In the clip, two women start kissing; this leads one of them to get out an ice cream sundae glass and poop in it. The other girl is getting horny as the girl drops her fecal matter into the glass. It comes out looking like soft serve. My first time watching that classic film, that gave *Citizen Kane* a run for its money, was at the very religious thrift store that graciously employed me.

Eve was Emily's sister. I viewed Emily as a motherly figure, so I was always respectful to her, but Eve was the apple of my eye. I used to talk disgustingly to Eve.

Phrases like, "Spray out your egg chunks at me," was the usual banter from me to her.

Eve would gripe to Emily, "I don't know why Travis talks so disgustingly with me when he treats you with respect."

Eve was crazy like me and was used to my unethical approach to my job. The thrift store had a black computer in the back that had a flatscreen—very fancy for that time period. It was used to print stickers and price tags for our donated items. The young employees would use the computer to check their Facebook pages because management didn't block any of those sites. I would go on my Facebook to talk to my girlfriend and friends.

My friend emailed me the link to *Two Girls, One Cup*. We watched the smut on the computer that employees used to track daily sales. It was the mid 2000s, so the term, "not appropriate for work" wasn't invented yet. When the girl pooped in the sundae glass, Eve and I were hooting and hollering. Customers were on the other side of the drywall while we watched girls make out with poop on their lips. It felt like a sin to be watching this indecency on the computer that helped Jesus Christ spread the message of giving back to others through donations and service.

911

It was a slow Saturday at the thrift store. I was playing pretend that I was the assistant manager because my pay didn't increase for my babysitting duties. I had to monitor a group of high school kids who were doing community service for truancy, weed, and curfew tickets. Nothing was really happening that day. I think that I might have smoked a little marijuana. We were taking bags of clothes out of cars, ripping the bags open, and dumping them in the blue laundry bins for sorting. There was a phone hanging on the wall right above where we dumped the clothes into the blue laundry bins. A lot of times the phone would go off the hook from the force of the clothes falling on the phone. It was a bad design flaw.

Anyway, with the phones, you had to dial 9 to get an outside line. I was pretty good with the phone and intercom system, so I was a fast dialer. On this day, I punched in, "911." Really fast on accident. My hands just slipped. I hung up right away. Moments later, the phone starts ringing off the hook.

I hear over the thrift store intercom, "Travis line one."

I picked up and the police were on the other end of the phone.

They say, "Is everything okay there at the store?"

I said, "Yes, I accidentally dialed 911 trying to get an outside line. I'm very sorry and I'm completely embarrassed."

There was a pause on the other end. Suddenly, the voice sizzles like bacon, "We have to stop out there to check things out. We need to make sure a robbery isn't taking place."

I flushed red with embarrassment. I replied, "For real?"

The donation area was located in our side parking lot off the main lot. We didn't have an overhead carport to keep people out of the rain as they donated to us. We would put up orange cones to guide the cars to pull up and turn around. I fully expected the small-town oinkers to show up. I was right.

Five minutes later, Oconomowoc police swarmed the donation area in their squads. I greeted them in the parking lot, where the cars pulled up to donate. I chitchatted with the police; meanwhile, another officer goes in to investigate. It doesn't take Sherlock Holmes long to discover that no money heist was taking place. The cops warned me about how fast I dial phone numbers, and they were back on to fight the big crimes of Oconomowoc, like riding your bicycle on the sidewalk or loitering.

As the emergency response vehicles left, I gazed next door at the strip mall in the process of being built. I pondered what life would be like for me when tenants moved in, and they could watch us walk out with our stolen goodies, taking them to our cars.

There was a big crime happening at the local thrift store, and it wasn't from me. There was a restaurant relocating to the strip mall that was being built next door to donations. My grandpa and I were concerned. The restaurant's large-ass windows in the dining hall would face the donations area. We were paranoid that Harry Peter would go have lunch there to spy on us. He would for sure be able to catch us stealing goodies while he lingered over his fries.

Harry Peter recently installed cameras outside the store to catch thieves. I remember telling my girlfriend Brittany, after the restaurant opened across the street, that I had staked out the location of the cameras. With knowledge of how the cameras were aimed, I would still be able to steal from the thrift store. One camera was by the donations door. Another one was in the back of the warehouse.

She got angry and said, "How about you stop stealing stuff? It's time to give it up!"

My thought was they had fucked me over by giving me a 10-cent raise, so I wasn't done punishing them for embarrassing me in front of my colleagues.

Time Theft

At the store, we would have to perform forklift feats. Daron was pulling a double pallet with two bales of cardboard. It was exactly the size and shape of the hallway he was pulling it through. It was the hallway where the volunteers signed in. Daron was scraping the sides, barely able to get through. My grandpa was watching him on the other end.

My grandpa said, "Schneider Trucking is looking for people like you, Daron."

That made me feel inadequate because the forklift gave me anxiety attacks.

My grandpa turned to me and said, "I'm leaving early today and you're going to clock me out at my normal time."

That was the first time that I committed time theft for my grandpa.

My grandpa and I had become addicted to stealing from the thrift store. We took stuff and sold it, we wiped our asses with toilet paper we lifted from the store, and now my grandpa made me start committing time theft. The store manager, Sid, was so gullible and complacent that when my grandpa started going home early Sid never even noticed.

My grandpa said, "If Sid is going to hide in his office all day and watch porn, I can go home early and have you clock me out!"

My grandpa can justify any fucked-up thing he does. My grandpa would leave at noon or around 2:00. He was supposed to stay until 5:00. My grandpa would call the store at exactly 4:58, and ask for me.

I would pick up, and he would say, "Go clock me out, boy!"

It was time to strip and wax the floors again. With Buck long gone, my grandpa damn sure wasn't going to stay overnight to wax the floors. My grandpa put me in charge of this onerous job that summer. My friend Brandon Evans was going to stay after on a Saturday to help with the dirty work.

Brandon was a deathcore guy who wore black heavy metal t-shirts. His hair was thinning pretty bad for his young age, but he was still quite the ladies' man. He had stretched ear lobes with black plugs in them. He was very skinny as death metal guys tend to be.

This time around waxing the floors was fun because I was with my buddy Brandon. Buck was gone, and I was in charge now. Brandon and I would listen to Psychosocial by Slipknot while we waxed the floors. He showed me all the deathcore that he liked.

Brandon and I would wax all night until he had to go to his job at the gas station. I would end up waxing by myself and clocking him out when I left. Committing a few hours of time theft for Brandon.

When I was a kid my grandpa would always say, "If you're ever stealing, act like you're supposed to be there." I would walk up confidently and clock my grandpa out in front of the assistant manager sometimes.

I started to get mad that my grandpa never clocked me out. Yet I was risking my job for him. Then he let me go to my girlfriend's house, so I could fuck her while on the clock. The best orgasm is the one you're getting paid for! The orgasmic time theft started going limp though. This one cashier, who I can't even picture, started to notice my routine of clocking my grandpa out.

The craziest part was that Sid confronted my grandpa and he lied about forgetting to clock out.

He elaborated on the flub and said, "I just didn't want to bother you to correct the time punch on the computer."

Sid was so stupid that he actually bought the lie and said, "Just make sure you're at the store from now on."

We were getting away with murder! I started to commit time theft in other ways too, when it came to my new junk removal business, The Junk Truck. I was hell bent on getting my junk removal company off the ground, but I still worked full time at the thrift store. I was getting a few jobs a week on my days off, but I wanted to be a full-time junk man. Luis the scrap man had been scrapping since the 1960's, but it was a side job for him. Luis worked at a factory in Waukesha that made bullets. No wonder, he wanted to put a bullet in my brain for stealing his scrap because he probably had an underground bunker at his house just filled with ammo. I was going to be a full-time junk man, unlike scrap man Luis. I definitely didn't want to work in a factory or even worse, join the union, like Donner preached. To market the junk business, I would load a bicycle in my car, and I'd drive to a subdivision, get on my bike, and pass flyers in new subdivisions around Oconomowoc. The thrift store was surrounded by an old subdivision, Misty Meadows, on the back side of the store. This would be the scene of my Junk Truck expansion. I would spread the word about my new junk removal service on the thrift store's dime. I would get paid to market my new-found career.

I would go at night to my mom's real estate office, and I'd print junk removal fliers when no one was looking. I would then bring them to the thrift store. When we had down time, I would borrow a bike from the store, and I would put fliers in mailboxes in Misty Meadows. I would take a quick ride back to find 3 or 4 cars waiting to be unloaded with donations. After they were taken care of, I would ride back and start doing flyers again.

Agnes lived in Misty Meadows, and she brought a flier in to show me that she had received it.

I was nervous because Sid saw it. He asked, "You're doing that on your own time, right?"

I nervously said, "Of course!"

My thought was that I wanted to get paid hourly for passing out the flyers, so it was just another instance of me committing time theft. We cooled down on time theft after that because it was becoming too risky.

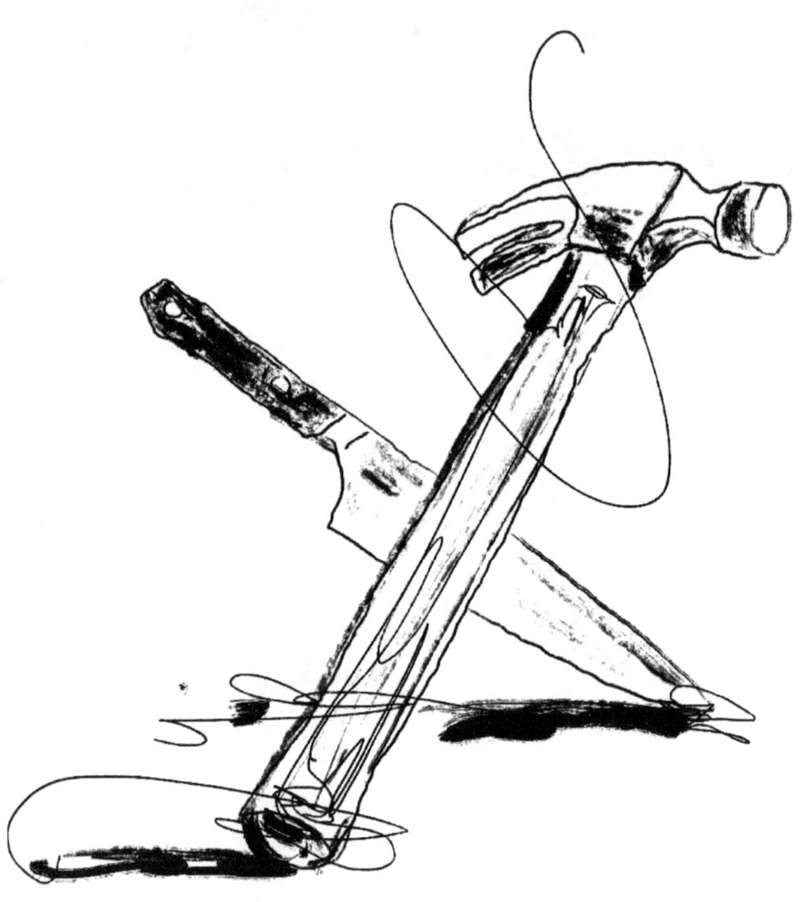

Hammers And Knives

I had a beautiful childhood friendship with a boy named Carey Mohawk. We would walk to this creek after school every day at the Oconomowoc Middle School. We would push each other in the creek and walk home soaked.

In our high school years, me, Carey, and his younger brother Ethan would get high during school every day. We would walk down to his house by the school and smoke. Sadly, after high school ended, Carey passed away from a drug overdose, so when his brother Ethan came looking for a job, I begged my grandpa to hire him.

Ethan was a short kid with albino skin. To top it off, he had almost white, blonde hair that he kept in a ponytail. He had acne scars on his face from when he was a teenager. Ethan always wore a white wife-beater shirt everywhere he went. On his feet was always a pair of sneakers. He always wore shorts that looked too big for him, like JNCO jeans were still in style.

Ethan's first week was interesting because during a shift he would turn, and say, "I'm gonna run home and take a shower!"

I would laugh and say, "Sure, go ahead."

Sid would ask where he was, so I would just always say the opposite end of the building from where we were at that moment. This would cause Sid to lose interest in finding Ethan because he was a lazy nitwit.

For entertainment purposes, Ethan and I would stand at one end of donations and throw claw hammers at the wall. We would try to see who could make the hammer stick; then we would go get a ladder and get it down. We were acting like lunatics, but something Ethan did one day was very uncalled for. During a slow time, Ethan threw the hammer through the wall and got the ladder out to grab the hammer. Suddenly, a geriatric volunteer shoved the door to donations open with her walker.

The old lady struggled to form the words, but she said, "What in God's name are you two boys doing? Wait until Harry Peter hears about this. You guys will lose your status as paid employees and you will have to do community service here at the store instead."

Ethan slowly pulled the hammer out of the drywall and climbed down the ladder. Ethan took one long look at her, and said, "Oh yeah, ya old bitch? If you love Jesus so much, I'll send you to heaven to meet the fucker!"

He started viciously beating the elderly volunteer with the claw hammer. Blood was splattering everywhere as the volunteer begged for her life, but Elliot wouldn't relent. As I saw the volunteer's brain matter, I thought that the game of hammers and knives had been taken too far. I did a double take at the inside of her brain because the brain was made up of drywall particles. I did a triple take as I shook off my daydream because that never happened. The volunteer didn't take the bloody beating, but the drywall of the thrift store did.

In reality, Ethan threw the hammer so hard that the head of the hammer was lodged in the drywall. Only the brown, wood handle was sticking out! We both fell over in laughter. Later on, Harry Peter noticed the circle holes in the drywall. He asked, "What's going on, Travis? Who is punching holes in the drywall up top there?"

I quickly improvised the line, "Harry, that is from when we put the ladder up. The ladder is putting holes in the wall."

Harry Peter looked befuddled. He didn't buy my bullshit but he couldn't think of any other explanation.

My grandpa would practice throwing knives in donations. He would throw knives at me; he would be laughing as I ran away. He would throw knives at the drywall. He kept donated knives that were good for throwing on a magnet strip, where he could grab them. He was really good at making a knife stick in the wall. I will never forget him, with a cigar in his mouth, throwing knives at the thrift store wall. He would spend all of our downtime, for a while, with a cigar hanging from his mouth and throwing knives at the drywall. He even put up paper that had a target he drew on it. There were all these little slits in the wall from this. Sid ended up talking to him. He made him take the targets down. My grandpa still didn't listen.

Crash and Burned

Because of my felony fleeing charge, I was on probation for two and a half years. This led to me keeping a marijuana smoking schedule. I would see my probation officer every two weeks. One visit would be at his office, and the other visit would be at my mom's house where I lived. I wouldn't smoke marijuana near the time that I had to go into his office, but before the time when he came to my house, I would smoke my brains out. I would usually smoke at work with Ethan, for I rarely kept weed at home during this time.

It was a beautiful day at the thrift store, and I just saw my devil probation officer at his office. Ethan and I were manning donations.

It was a slow donation day, so Ethan asked me, "Do you want to smoke?"

"Fuck yes!"

We headed through the sorting room, walked through the electronics room, and turned left out the steel door by the dumpsters. Ethan and I stepped behind the compactor and he pulled out the craziest weed I had ever seen.

This was 2009 in Wisconsin, so I had rarely seen medical marijuana. Ethan pulled out a Sherlock pipe and packed it with the herb. We both took fat rips off the pipe until I was in a comatose state. After we smoked, we left the scene of the crime. I immediately had the munchies, so I grabbed the keys to my grandpa's white van that just so happened to have a white skeleton for a passenger. My grandpa put a skeleton in the passenger seat of his van to ride around with. It was a rubber skeleton that looked like it had rotting flesh, for Halloween season. I would be going to the bank on my day off, and I'd see my grandpa out and about town driving the van with a bloody skeleton as his passenger. It would always crack me up.

There was a newly built Kwik Trip across the street, so I went there for some snacks. I should not have been driving because I was very stoned. I pulled into a front parking spot and went inside for snacks. I came out, hopped in the van, and turned the ignition. Without looking behind me, I started to back out. CRASH! My body was jerked forward as I backed into the car behind me! I heard someone start bitching. I jumped out and saw Cody Vullmer Sr. looking at a minor scratch on his blue car. He was a teacher at Oconomowoc High School. He also had a son with Down syndrome, who was one of the football coaches at the school. Both Codys were beloved at my school. I wasn't being beloved by Cody Vullmer Sr. now.

The first thing he said was, "We need to file a police report."

It was just a tiny little scratch on his car! I could not deal with the cops because I was so stoned, so we exchanged information. I drove back and confessed to my grandpa that I got in an accident with his van. I gave Mr. Vullmer my grandpa's number and told him to call him.

That day I was a complete wreck; I kept telling my grandpa, "He didn't file a police report at all, so let's just deny it!"

My grandpa said, "We have to fix his bumper because he leased the car. I also don't have insurance on that van, Travis!"

My grandpa never carried insurance on any of his vehicles, ever, in his whole life. My grandpa had Cody get a couple of quotes. Even though it was just a tiny scratch, they had to replace the bumper and a few car panels to match the blue paint.

My grandpa was so pissed, and bitched to Cody, "It's a tiny little scratch! Travis shouldn't have to pay for it!"

Cody still forced us to pay out of pocket for the scratch on the bumper. I look back on that day and I should not have been smoking and driving. I'm just glad that I didn't hurt anyone or back my car over a baby.

The Vending Machine

Ethan and I were causing all kinds of commotion at the store and in life. We were throwing hammers through the wall, smoking pot behind the compactor, and crashing vans into cars while stoned. We were definitely punk-ass kids. My mom's generation called people like us *dirtballs*. She would use this term when she referred to people from her high school. We were just beginning to be bastards, which may have been a step up.

The store had a break room that was upstairs. A local guy provided vending machine services. He would come in a van stocked with cans of soda and candy. Upstairs he put one very outdated soda machine and one very outdated candy machine. He also had a candy dispenser that you would put 25 cents in and turn a knob. You used to see them in Kmart lobbies (Kmarts were department stores where you could buy a pair of jeans, a microwave, and new bedding, then stop for a slice at the in-store Little Cesar's pizza).

I slowly became friends with the guy over time. It would be dead at the store, and I would shoot the shit with the vending machine guy. Now like I said, Ethan and I were on a path of destruction. We figured out that we could jam our hand up through the face of the machine and pull out Snickers bars. It worked great for the first few candy bars, but the further back ones were impossible to get at.

One day, I really wanted a Snickers, so I forced my hand in the machine and broke the faceplate off. Instead of being honest, we raided the machine for all the candy. We didn't take it all at once; we just didn't tell anybody that it broke. At our leisure, we ate all the candy before the vending machine guy returned to restock the machines. We even broke open the top of the Kmart style dispenser and ate all the candy out of that, too. That machine had Mike and Ike's, M&Ms, and Hot Tamales in it. When the candy guy came, I was sweating bullets. I was so nervous. I usually talked to him, so I made sure to keep up my act.

He looked puzzled at the candy machine and said, "Someone broke into my machine and got everything!"

I said, "Really? We have a lot of volunteers coming through here. I bet it was one of them!"

He agreed with me and I sighed in relief. He then asked me, "Do you think you could keep an eye up here in the break room? They broke the lock off of this machine and it's so old that I don't know where to find a replacement."

At that moment, I felt like the biggest piece of shit. It was one thing to steal from the store, but now I was messing with some mom-and-pop shop. I told Ethan that it was wrong what we did. The vending machine guy ended up jerry-rigging the lock to stay closed. We didn't ever steal candy again because I felt so bad. Ethan didn't feel bad though.

The Grease Guys

My Grandpa had zero hiring experience, so the first set of guys that would walk through the door for a donations gig always got the job. Two guys showed up to get work. One was a husky short guy with a greasy, dirty-blonde ponytail, CV Joint. The other guy was a redneck with a chipped tooth. Chipped Tooth wore a 1990s Wisconsin Badgers sweater a lot. They claimed to be roommates, have reliable transportation, and would show up every day. The two guys had night jobs, but they were looking for day work. They would work at the thrift store during the day and would degrease restaurant hood vents at night. When they would talk about grease, you could see a boner rise in both their jeans. They couldn't get enough fast food grease! They were putting in a hard night's work! On their first day of work, we noticed that Chipped Tooth was a good worker, but CV Joint was a scuzzy slacker.

CV Joint was a middle-aged fat guy with greasy hair. One of his two front teeth was rotten and black. He always sat around smoking Newport menthol cigarettes. CV Joint would sit down a lot and choke down off-brand menthol cigarettes. He drove an old souped-up Honda that ran like shit.

CV would puff on a grit and say, "I really shouldn't be driving that because I need to get the CV joint fixed on the car."

He would never do any work when a car would pull up to donations. I would be hauling the bags in, ripping them open, and rough sorting the contents. CV Joint would be amusing himself with a McDonald's toy that lay on the table.

On the other hand, there was Chipped Tooth. He was quite the character. A taller redneck, he looked inbred. He kept his brown hair short on top. He dressed in "I never left my hometown" clothes. One of his two front teeth was badly chipped and was rotting out of his head.

Chipped Tooth would blast butt rock in his silver 1990's Ford Taurus before his shift. One time, I came out the donation door to find Chipped Tooth smoking a cigarette in his car blasting Linkin Park. I caught Chipped Tooth pretending to hold a mic and scream the lyrics to Linkin Park's "One Step Closer." He was channeling Chester Bennington as he held his ghost mic and screamed the words, "SHUT UP WHEN I'M TALKING TO YOU!"

When I was in second grade, we had a substitute teacher. I spent the day at school, pretending to be in the band Nirvana. I kept playing air guitar, but we had to go to art class soon. My substitute teacher embarrassed me by saying, "Travis! It's time to put the guitar away!"

Now, what Chipped Tooth was doing at the thrift store looked really goofy because he was far from a kid; he was in his 40s at this point. He lived with a married couple. The husband owned the grease business. The husband, CV Joint, and Chipped Tooth would climb the roofs of fast food restaurants and remove the grease from the hood vents of the fryers. They would use these very toxic acids to eat and scrub away at the grease buildup in the hood vent. The crew would wear old jeans that they got from the thrift store. Chipped Tooth was the husband's right-hand man.

Chipped Tooth claimed to be the brother of the wife. The wife was pudgy and almost resembled an albino. She had a 1980s hairstyle, bleached blonde hair. Chipped Tooth would always bring her back and say, "I have the best sister, guys!" They would hang out together in the donation room, smoke cigarettes, and take in the donations when needed.

Something weird happened one day between Chipped Tooth and his sister. On that fateful day, I was back by the baler working on tying a bale of clothes together. My grandpa was manning the standup forklift to stack the bricks of clothes to be picked up at a later date. We finished and walked past electronics, through the sorting room, and into the back room of the old Piggly Wiggly. The retired volunteers would be hard at work sorting and pricing clothes.

The room at the end is the donation room. It still has the grocery store circle window doors that led from the stockroom to the cooler. Now the doors led from the sorting room to donations. As my grandpa and I looked through the circle window door, we saw Chipped Tooth sloppily tongue-kissing his sister! I took one look at my grandpa and we started laughing hysterically. Nasty redneck was porking his sister! My grandpa confronted Chipped Tooth about this.

My grandpa said, "You're nasty, kissing your sister like that!"

He looked embarrassed and said, "She isn't really my sister. She's my grease boss's wife; she's like a sister to me though."

My grandpa giggled, and said, "Then why the fuck are you smooching her?"

He replied, "I'm having an affair with her. We live together, so it's complicated."

Not only was he committing adultery, but he was committing adultery with his sister, in Jesus' eyes! It all goes back to thoughts-words-deeds!

They lived above a local bar called Wingers. Eventually my grandpa couldn't stand CV Joint's lazy ass and he canned him. Chipped Tooth went, too. Years later, I saw Chipped Tooth shopping at a Spirit Halloween I worked at.

I checked him out and he told me, "I ended up going to work for the Waukesha thrift store. I worked at the dock there until I got sick of it."

It was nice to see him. He introduced me to his wife, and it was nice to find out that it wasn't his sister.

The Fraudster

There was something magnetic about the thrift store. We just attracted oddballs who wanted to do community service with us. One day, this skinny fellow in a MercyMe baseball hat showed up to do some community service. He told my grandpa that he wanted to work off some hours of his mandatory community service sentence. He introduced himself as Trevor.

He always had a small Yorkshire terrier following him around. She was just a tiny little thing. You could tell that the dog was his only friend. When Trevor met us, he told us that he was a man of faith.

Trevor said, "I'm a Christian, and I'm heavily involved in my church."

Honestly, Trevor seemed like a huge dork, so I didn't think much of him. The more I got to know him, the weirder his lifestyle was for me to grasp. At first Trevor just seemed like your average Kool Aid drinker, but the layers to his onion began to peel. Once Trevor was peeled, I couldn't quite figure out what to make of him.

First off, Trevor drove a brand-new red Dodge Ram truck equipped with very expensive, custom Dub Rims. They were the type of rims that required a custom-fitted wrench to get them off; this was so no one could take the wheels. Trevor was very bad with money, judging by the new red Dodge Truck.

He said, "I love to go to the movies. I see a movie at the theater every day."

I asked, "Doesn't that get expensive?"

Trevor replied, "I don't care. I love watching stories."

Trevor was recently retired, so he spent a lot of time putting in community service hours at the thrift store. Harry Peter loved Trevor because he portrayed himself as a man of God. Trevor was always talking about how he loved the church band that performed at the church he attended.

Trevor said, "MercyMe is my favorite Christian band; I have seen them several times."

I will be honest. I made fun of Trevor for his religious views. I was an atheist who liked to mock religion. It's something that I regret. At the time, I was a young idiot who had a warped view of the world. I was cruel and unusual to him. We would get into arguments about his faith. I thought he was a total dweeb for being involved in church.

I would walk up to him and say, "I want to fuck my mother."

He thought I was so strange.

I amped up my psychotic behavior: "I suck Jesus Christ's cock!"

He would say, "You are a little punk kid!"

Again, as a man in my thirties now I am completely embarrassed by the actions of my younger days. Trevor knew that I was an immature adolescent.

Now, this is where the dude gets weird. My grandpa also thought there was something off with Trevor. You see, people tend to let their guard down around my grandpa and me, mostly because of how openly real we are and how fucked up we act. In any moral hierarchy, we'd be at the bottom. So people assume we wouldn't judge them.

As we took in donations together, he admitted that his community service was court ordered.

Supposedly, he committed insurance fraud by saying that his truck was stolen. He had a friend keep the truck in a garage and was eventually caught.

He said, "The insurance company hired a private investigator to find out what really happened to the truck. My lies started to unravel from there."

My grandpa asked him, "How can you be a Christian and commit insurance fraud?"

(The guy still claimed to be a Christian.)

He replied, "I have been forgiven for my sins."

My grandpa and I would make fun of him behind his back. I didn't like him bringing his dog to work, and I really hated having to listen to him sing along to the Christian rock the store played over the loudspeakers. Trevor also had another aspect to his Christianity that was bizarre. He loved to smoke medical marijuana. It was the late 2000's, and medical marijuana was unheard of in Southeastern Wisconsin. Trevor always said, "I smoke nothing but the good shit!"

I said, "Bring some into work sometime."

Looking back, I smoked ditch weed, compared to what he was about to bring into the thrift store. When he showed me his herb, I had never seen gas like that before. The weed was covered in crystals, hairs, and smelled medical. I had only seen weed like this in *High Times* magazine . . . in the centerfold! We went out by the compactors to smoke his bud. I remember being so high that it was hard to unload vehicle donations the rest of the day.

As we got more acquainted with each other Trevor told me his life story. He had worked most of his life at A.L. Smith, a big manufacturer in Milwaukee that made truck frames. Trevor told me that he was forced to retire from A.L. Smith because he was selling weed out of his locker at work.

"All my coworkers knew that I had the bomb weed, so I would have a line at my locker on pay day."

We started to become really close because I valued anyone that had the kind of weed that he possessed. I was so shallow back then. I had spent my entire youth and young adulthood being kind of an asshole. In 2022, I got sober . . . only to realize how horrible of a person I had been. I should have shown this guy respect at first, when I just thought he was an oddball. My sobriety has put me on a quest to right the wrongs of my past. I will be doing quality control work until the day I die.

Couches For Cash

My grandpa would stage sections in our furniture showroom area. It would look like when they show a bedroom set on *The Price Is Right*. He had me mopping in between the different living room, dining room, or bedroom scenes when I sat down to take a break.

I sat on a couch that had a matching love seat, and a guy sat across from me and said, "I love the couch I'm sitting on, but it's too expensive!"

I had a shit-eating grin on my face and said, "There is always a cash price! Listen, you give me 40 bucks and I'll help you load it in your car!"

"Sounds good to me because 80 bucks is way too much for used furniture!"

I told the guy to pull around to the side of the donations building. I used a flatbed cart to haul the couches to his gray beat-down van. He handed me 40 bucks cash, and I pocketed the bills instantly.

I went back to the donation room and noticed someone had donated a SpongeBob Squarepants costume. I wore the costume the rest of the day unloading cars. The problem was that it wasn't anywhere near Halloween. Customers were weirded out when a guy came out of the donations area in a big SpongeBob costume to take in their stuff.

I went up to the front of the store to shoot the shit with the girls at the register. I shouldn't have been up there, but I was bored in the donation room. A woman came through the checkout lane with women's clothes. I started to fold the clothes and put them in a plastic bag for her.

The woman said, in a snarky tone, "I want a woman to bag my garments. You're making me uncomfortable."

I said, "I'm sorry, ma'am."

She shot back, "Don't call me 'ma'am!'"

I was uncomfortable, so I walked back to the donation room, still in costume and all. I wore the costume home, and my mom took a photo of me. My parents had a fenced yard with a long walkway. My mom saw me heading towards the house as SpongeBob. She ran out to snap a picture with a giant grin. That is still a very warm memory for me, when I look at the picture. I have a giant smile on my face with my hands in the air.

Later that night, I went and did drugs at a friend's house wearing the SpongeBob costume. I ended up giving the costume to a girl named Stephanie Katon.

I was really high and I said, "I don't want this costume anymore. Does anybody want it?"

Stephanie in a shy tone said, "I want it!"

I gave the costume to Stephanie Katon at the party that night. Years later, Stephanie passed away. I was looking at her profile after her death, and I stumbled on pictures of her wearing the SpongeBob costume at other parties she went to. It made me feel good to know that her parents probably saw those pictures after her death and wondered where the hell she got such a goofy costume. I hope the pictures of Stephanie in the SpongeBob costume made them smile as they grieved over their daughter's sudden death.

Video Game Nerd

Daron was fired around this time because he was caught smoking pot behind the dumpsters with two female cashiers.

One Saturday, Daron got the urge to smoke weed with these two cashiers.

He said, "We should just wait till after work, it's not good to smoke at the thrift store during work hours."

It was wintertime, so the compactor had snow behind it. They couldn't take cover like we usually did when we were smoking in non-winter months. A new cashier came out to ask a question as Daron and the other two girls were passing the pipe around.

The new cashier said, "Hey! I know that smell! It's cool, don't worry!"

But this new cashier turned around and tattled on them. Originally when the new cashier narced them out, she just mentioned the two girls, Andrea and Tara. Andrea didn't know that Daron wasn't mentioned, so she went up to the office with the round windows to plead for all three of their jobs. Now that they knew Daron was included in the bad behavior, they ended up firing him as well. Years later, Daron told me that his resume said that he worked from March 2007 through February 2009. It was definitely sad to see him go.

Now that Daron was gone, we ended up hiring the first people that showed up. Baby Huey was a hangaround who started off doing community service at the store. He was a tall, fat kid who was a pretty decent worker. Baby Huey looked like a bull in a china shop. He had light brown hair with a little bit of acne on his cheeks. My grandpa called him Baby Huey because he looked like the 1950s cartoon character, a dumb duckling, freakishly huge, that would break something just by being near it.

Our Baby Huey was from Peoria, Illinois, so he didn't know a lot of people around the Lake Country area. He was one of those introverts that liked to play video games all day and stuff their face with gas-station delights.

I myself had a little side business of selling video games at that time. Tucked away behind the blue bins that lined the shelves, I stored Rubbermaid totes that held video games. I would put every DVD, video game, and gaming system in the tote. When the tote was full of media, I would drive it three doors down from our store to the video store. They would give me good money for the stolen loot. I did this routine a good number of times up until Baby Huey started working in donations.

Baby Huey wanted to confiscate games too, but that would be cutting into my video game racket, so I would always try to work the donations door to grab the games first. Lo and behold, Baby Huey found my stash of games behind the blue bins and he started rummaging through it one day. I came in and saw him and got all pissed.

"That is my stuff!" I shouted.

He stated, "Then take it home. Why let it sit here?"

He was right, so every time a video game came in, I would run it right out to my windowless Corolla. This was 2009, so we rarely saw Playstation 2s get donated since they were new to the market. A pristine expansion-bay PlayStation 2 came in and Baby Huey got to it first. He set it aside to steal later. I fucking needed that Playstation, so when he went out to put sports equipment away, I hid the PlayStation for myself. He came back to check on his game console, and I just acted dumb.

He started throwing stuff around in a rage looking for the PS2 like a madman.

He said in anger, "Why did you take my PS2?"

I just played dumb, which made him not like me anymore.

He got upset, and said, "That PS2 meant a lot to me. It had a special graphics card in it."

I let him feel sorrow. He looked forever for that PS2, he got dangerously close to its hiding spot. He recruited me to help him look for the stolen game console, which made me feel weird. After his shift, I put the PS2 in my trunk.

It was a terrible thing to do. I was very greedy back then; I think back and feel sad that I did that to Huey. Today, I am not a thief at all, but in my past, I was something fucking else! I sent him a friend request on Facebook years later and he denied my request. I have learned that people remember you for your actions not your words.

As my aunt says, "People won't remember what you said, but they'll remember how you made them feel."

I hope Baby Huey is doing really well in life. I hope he is happy.

Gasoline

I held my grandpa in high esteem for the wise man that he was. I always viewed my grandpa as this wise man who was the holder of all knowledge. I put him on a pedestal thinking that he never made mistakes. When I was a kid, I felt that he was the perfect man, even though he was the most messed up person I knew. The first time I saw my grandpa make a big mistake was at the thrift store.

A car pulled up to donations. In the pile of crap they offered as a donation we discovered a gas can. My grandpa shook the gas can to ascertain that it was empty only to discover that it still had gasoline in it. My grandpa took the cap off, dumped the gasoline out all over the ground, and tossed the gas can in the blue laundry bin that we used as a trash can.

Now, if you know anything about oil spills, they can be really slick. You'll see when watching Nascar races that they put granular diatomaceous earth down when there's an oil spill. That's because oil spills are slippery. That day, it was close to 4:00 PM when my grandpa left for the day. It was a Friday afternoon, my grandpa didn't work weekends. This would leave me to take care of business in donations on that following Saturday.

The next morning, cars were pulling up to give us their donations. A car would pull up, the person would get out, and they would almost slip on the gasoline spill. Everyone kept complaining about it.

One customer said, "You need to get that oil slick taken care of because I almost took a digger."

I was with Baby Huey that day.

He said, "Don't worry about it! We will take care of it at some point."

Another customer pulled up, got out, and they almost fell on their ass!

The customer complained, "Please take care of that oil slick because I almost fell down!"

Huey again just shrugged them off. He said, "Don't worry about it. Thank you for your donation!"

That customer left mad. The last customer to complain almost slipped on her butt.

She got mad and said, "You need to call the fire department because that oil slick isn't safe!"

Baby Huey again just shrugged her away.

He said, "Don't worry about it, ma'am."

She said, "No, I am worried about it!" She then took off in her car.

Ten minutes later, a giant yellow fire truck showed up at the donations parking lot. A firefighter got out with a huge sack of kitty litter. He dumped it on the ground.

The firefighter said, "Someone just called saying that you guys had an oil slick that needed to be defused. It is a danger to your customers to have a parking lot like this."

I was embarrassed that we told all those customers not to worry about it. I could have put one of them in danger. I remember feeling for the first time that my grandpa wasn't perfect. That Monday, Sid came to donations to yell at us about the oil slick. He interrogated us about who dumped the gasoline.

Sid said, "Who would be such an idiot as to dump gasoline on the ground?"

My grandpa was red in the face with embarrassment as he lied through his teeth.

He replied, "I bet it was those damn military school kids!"

Sid believed my grandpa because he was a dumbass. After Sid left, my grandpa went outside to enjoy a cigar.

He turned to me and said, "See, Travis! Even in my old age, I still make mistakes. That was a really stupid move, grandson. I am always still learning."

That weekend taught me that we are all humans who make mistakes from time to time.

Stacy

Sid had hired a woman named Stacy. She walked funny, and she looked like a goose. Stacy was a short woman in her early 30s. She was Caucasian with white-blonde hair. Stacy walked with a weird limp, almost like she had a muscle disorder. She had a look that screamed, "I was an 80s mall rat." I found her strangely hot, even though I was 15 years her junior. She always wore a blue T-shirt with her thrift store lanyard that showed her name to customers.

She was very quiet at first. That was until Sid made her assistant manager; I could tell Sid secretly wanted to be with Stacy. He was always near her when she was sorting clothes in the big room that used to be the back warehouse of Piggly Wiggly.

Emily had since divorced her teacher husband and started dating this young fuckboy. He was in school to be an airplane mechanic, so they had to move far up north to Oshkosh, Wisconsin. That town is a mecca for the airline industry, as it hosts the EAA Air Show. Emily had accepted a position at GoodWill in Oshkosh as a manager. This made the assistant manager position open for quiet Stacy to take.

The second Stacy became the assistant manager, she became power-hungry. She started to involve herself in every aspect of the store. She became very separated from the workers that she once called friends.

Stacy and I vibed on Ozzy a lot. Stacy's first concert was Ozzy Osbourne's The Ultimate Sin Tour with Metallica as the opener. I thought she was cool until she rose to take charge; she started bossing us around.

My grandpa, who didn't take direction well, would call Stacy a "pig fucking whore" behind her back. We would smoke cigs in donations and mock how fucking stupid Stacy was. But Stacy and Sid were a thrift store power couple now; she might be onto us.

Nap Time

Have you ever seen the episode of *Seinfeld* where George sets up a bed under his desk in his office at Yankee Stadium? George arranges a little room under his desk to nap, with all the amenities. I always loved that premise as a child, when I would watch the show with my dad. George's desk seemed like a cool treehouse for adults. I wanted one of my own when I grew up.

The time had now come. I was a burnout working at a thrift store. I was always tired at work because I would smoke weed behind the dumpsters. This made me want to lay down. I fondly remembered that episode, George making his secret sleeping spot. I thought that I could do the same.

In the back warehouse of the store there was an area that Harry Peter constructed to house the out-of-season clothes. If it was the cold weather season, the racks would be full of short-sleeved clothes. If it was hot out, the racks would hold the long-sleeved clothing. This was so we could hold onto the good stuff that was currently out of season. The clothes rack was made out of 2X4's and metal rods. The off-season clothes rack was all the way in the back of the warehouse, tucked away where there was a bunch of furniture stacked up . . . blocking the view. The rack was always full of garments, so there was plenty of cover.

This would be the site of my secret sleeping area, my treehouse, my nap burrow. I didn't go all out like George. I just arranged a bunch of clothes in the form of a pillow and took a blanket in there, in the space between the 2X4s. I would then slide the hanging clothes over the bunched-up clothes lying on the ground. You couldn't tell that the items were there waiting for my slumber because the racks were bursting with clothes. I would commit time theft by sleeping for a few hours when donations were slow.

In the *Seinfeld* episode, George gets caught sleeping under his desk because he has an alarm clock there. His boss Steinbrenner hears the ticking of the alarm clock and thinks it's a bomb. Steinbrenner calls in the bomb squad and they dismantle George's desk.

Eventually, I got lackadaisical like George. I wouldn't clean up the clothes after my naps, causing Stacy to discover my makeshift bedchamber. She asked me to come to the back and showed me the pile of clothes.

She said, "Travis, I think someone was sleeping back here!"

I nodded sagely, said, "Hmmm," and acted like this was a new revelation to me. Stacy partially took me back there because she knew I was sleeping there, but Stacy couldn't prove it. She told me about her finding, and I made sure to never sleep at work again. In the last part of the *Seinfeld* episode, George misses his desk bed, so he sleeps in Jerry's cupboards. I made sure to go home and sleep in my walk-in closet to be like George.

Secret Santa

It was the holiday season, and Sid thought that it would be fun to exchange Secret Santa gifts. I don't remember who got my name in the drawing, but I sure remember who I picked. I ended up getting paired up with Sid to get him a gift.

I thought to myself, "*Fuck! Sid hates my guts. Out of every employee at the store, how did I pick Sid's name and become his Secret Santa?*"

I didn't like Sid at all, but I wanted to do good on my part. I wanted to actually get him a gift he liked for the holiday season.

He kept saying, "I hope Stacy picked my name!"

He had a huge crush on Stacy, so Sid hoped that she would give him the gift of her wet vagina. This sadly wasn't going to be the case for him. Sid had the same routine every day. He would watch porn in his office until he got bored of it, then he would come down to the donation area to bum a smoke from us. We were allowed to smoke cigarettes in the donation room. Sid would never buy a pack of his own cigarettes. He was acting like we were growing fields of tobacco and had an endless supply of cigarettes.

He would sit in donations and smoke our cigarettes all day while he yapped about bullshit he knew nothing about. He was a know-it-all, as well as being completely stingy. Sid also had a habit of saying that he was quitting smoking.

He used to say, "Quitting cigarettes is easy; I've quit 1,000 times!"

I thought it would be funny if I bought him a pack of cigarettes for his Secret Santa gift. I went across the street to Kwik Trip, bought the cigarettes he favored, and headed back to wrap up the Camel

Lights. I came back from the store with his favorite cancer sticks. I also thought it would be funny to duct tape the tiny pack of cigarettes inside a humongous box, so it would appear like there was nothing in the box. I got the biggest box I could find, taped the cigarettes to the bottom of the box, and wrapped the gift the best I could.

All the employees exchanged gifts that very day. Sid came back to the donations area to open his giant gift-wrapped box. My grandpa and I were eager to watch him open the gift.

Sid shook the box and said, "What the fuck? There's nothing in this box!"

We both said to Sid, "No, something's in there, so open it already!"

Sid unwrapped the gift, opened the box and saw the cigarettes, then instantly turned an angry red. He blurted out, "Who the fuck got me these cigarettes? I'm going to fire them!" The gift had backfired on me. It was one of those situations where the gift symbolized the truth, and the truth sometimes hurts. Sid took the gift as an insult because he knew that he bummed cigarettes off of every smoker all the time. He demanded to know who his Secret Santa was.

I fessed up to being his Secret Santa, and – surprise, surprise – he was completely disgusted with me. This was just another reason for Sid to hate my existence.

My grandpa calmed him down by saying, "It was just a joke, Sid, don't take it so literally."

He said, "This isn't funny! I'm supposed to be quitting smoking. This is how you treat someone who is trying to quit?"

My grandpa calmed him down, but that was another notch on the long belt of Sid hating me.

The Fight

The holy one, Harry Peter, worked out a deal with a furniture company that was going out of business. All the donation guys were guessing whether the furniture would be worth a damn. The liquidated company was going to ship a semi-trailer to sit outside. The donations team was going to sell furniture right out of the trailer. I was excited to see what we were dealing with. The trailer arrived, and it was beat to shit. The furniture was all really old and outdated.

My grandpa complained, "This stuff is all junk!"

The old saying goes, "One man's junk is another man's treasure." People actually were interested in sifting through this crap. We would let customers look around in the trailer, and people were actually buying the chairs. Sid wanted us to have the customers pick out the chairs, walk around the building, go back inside, and pay for them. The customers were annoyed at this idea, so my grandpa and I started selling the chairs out the trailer and pocketing the money.

Cameron was working that day too, so we had to cut him in on the cash. Cameron was my friend from early in my high school career. We used to make skate and BMX videos together. People bought so much of the crappy furniture that we had to shift the furniture around in the trailer to make it look full. My grandpa was stacking chairs, so I thought I would bust his balls.

I said, "I love your rival motorcycle gang."

Without hesitation my grandpa threw one of the chairs towards my face. I just got out of the way fast enough to escape decapitation. No flies on grandpa. He still had the stuff.

Cameron thought my grandpa was a badass because of his spooky tales of being a biker.

We were selling the chairs for two bucks apiece. The money added up, but I was greedy, so I started pocketing my own side money. My grandpa and Cameron questioned the amount of money we were making; I gave them an answer, an odd number, and they said, "The money should be in an even amount." They were right, if each chair brought in two bucks, the take should have been an even number.

I coughed up the money and we unwrinkled all the ones in our pockets. We looked like guys at a strip club. I was a terrible mathematician and an even worse criminal. How could I forget that we were selling an item for two bucks? Why wouldn't I spit out an even dollar amount for our take of the loot?

I reluctantly handed over all the cash to my grandpa and Cameron. It was so competitive to steal stuff and sell it, it felt like such a great game, that I was becoming blind with greed. (My current status? I've changed. I am now extremely poor and fear being greedy like that again. I resolved that money is just paper. What matters is spending time with my grandpa in his last years. Money doesn't matter to me now.) But it sure did then!

My grandpa was my role model in life. I couldn't count on my dad because he suffered from alcoholism. I always yearned for his love, but he was unavailable, so what I needed was for my grandpa to think that I was a badass —like him. My grandpa didn't view me as a tough guy though. He viewed me as an artist, which is what I eventually became. At the time, I desperately wanted him to see me as someone who could hold my own in a fight.

When I stayed with my grandpa, I bought the new Ozzy album, *Black Rain.* I drove around in my Corolla and blasted the new tunes. I was driving really fast past a house, and there was a high schooler playing with his kid brother.

He yelled, "Slow down!"

I flipped him off and pulled over. The red-headed high schooler ended up punching me in the face. I took off, but his mother called the cops on me. She reported my license plate. That's how my grandpa found out. My grandpa was ashamed of me.

He said, "You got beat up by a high schooler, Travis. Why didn't you fight back?"

My grandpa had been involved in a plethora of bar brawls during his time with the motorcycle gang, so I really let him down by getting sucker punched. That event with the high schooler haunted me for years. I wanted my grandpa to think of me as a tough guy. That came to fruition when an old friend got hired at the thrift store.

I got my grandpa to hire Cameron for a few days a week. Instantly, I realized why I had stopped hanging out with Cameron. He was so cocky about everything. If you told a story, he would have to one-up your story. If you had a car, he had a better car.

Cameron liked to push your buttons and expect zero reaction. One time I was on the phone, and he kept slapping me on the chest in a playful way. It was getting on my nerves. After the millionth slap to my chest, to be funny, I fake punched him on the chin. My depth perception was off and my fist slightly brushed his chin. Because Cameron was such a beguiled little asshole who couldn't take a joke, he blew up in a rage.

I got off the phone, and said, "Cameron! I am so sorry!"

He started to gather his stuff to leave. I didn't want it to end like this, so I pleaded with him. My grandpa showed up and was confused by Cameron's demeanor. Just then a car pulled up to donate a circular laundry basket full of clothes riding in the backseat. I opened the car door and grabbed the full basket.

At that very moment, Cameron walked outside, and said, "See you later, Travis! You never were shit anyway!"

I instantly threw the basket, and I started walloping Cameron with my fists. Clothes and fists went flying! I broke the skin on Cameron's nose, he made it to his car to regroup before speeding off.

My grandpa said, "Atta boy! I'm so proud of you for kicking that kid's ass!"

It was a good feeling to finally be accredited in the eyes of my badass, biker grandpa! I was finally tough enough in my grandpa's eyes! The weird part was that I kept my job. I beat up an employee in front of a patron. They decided to fire Cameron because my grandpa talked them into supporting nepotism. I absolutely should have been fired in that situation, but I had an angel watching over me.

Zero Donations

My grandpa, during one period of his employment at the thrift store, was always very rude to the customers. I hated my job so much, too. Taking in people's trash and having to spend so much time throwing the donations in the compactor was wearing me thin. I started to lash out at customers and regularly worked in a blind rage.

This one time, my grandpa and I were mean to a female patron. This woman pulled up and we opened her car door to grab bags of clothes. I gave her a big attitude about her load of donations. My grandpa came out and gave her the speech about how we didn't take this and that.

The woman said, "You guys seem like you hate your fucking jobs!"

I said, "We do hate our jobs."

She said, "You can always quit! You don't have to work here. No one is forcing you."

In some ways she was right, but I felt trapped at the thrift store because it was a cool job that let me slack off. It would be hard to go out into corporate America to work for the man. I would never have it as easy as at the thrift store.

Once a customer bought a computer desk that was made of cheap particle board. He drove around, handed me the slip, and I angrily went to retrieve the desk with a volunteer. I picked it up the wrong way and started off backwards with the desk. It was so cheap that it fell apart right in front of the customer. I was so pissed off that I just shrugged my shoulders and stormed off. I looked like a fool to whoever that customer was. They probably were thinking " *What a dickhead.*" I absolutely was.

Summer was a tough time for us because it brought tension. Patrons were told that their donations were pure shit. We were in the height of the church rummage sale season. Local churches would hold giant rummage sales, and then all the garbage that didn't sell would be hauled to the thrift store to be donated. I will let you in on a little secret about what would happen next. We wouldn't be able to sell any of the crap from the church, so we would then spend the next hour throwing all the donations in the compactor. Oh joy!

One Friday afternoon, a guy pulled up with a flat snowmobile trailer piled up to the brim with crap. It looked like every item had sat outside for years: most of the items were sun-bleached. The guy hopped out of his truck.

My grandpa took one look and said, "We don't want it."

The guy asked, "And why not?"

My grandpa smirked and said, "This is all garbage!"

The guy was offended that the junk he hoped to dump on us was being rejected. The guy could have gotten out of his truck, taken a dump, and he still would be offended he couldn't donate his turds to us. The guy copped an attitude, and I just lost it. I threw up my fists, and I told him to fucking fight me. I know it's insane to try and beat up one of your customers, but I am a maniac. The guy backed off and demanded to speak to Sid.

Sid was so pissed at my grandpa and I, but we were sick of having to spend hours loading the dumpster with shit people dumped on us. For some reason, Sid didn't fire us for the 100th time. We were starting to get a bad reputation with the thrift store's customers because of our attitudes. To be honest, I was burned out by working at the thrift store and getting asked stupid questions. We only had a good attitude when something we could steal came in. I was turning into a thrift store monster.

Someone would pull up, my grandpa would come out with a cigar in his mouth, and he'd treat the person with disrespect. My grandpa and I had a bad reputation around town. During donation hours, there would usually be a steady flow of cars all day. Then cars stopped showing up after word got out that we were turning away half of everything that people brought to us. We stopped getting cars pulling up. Word around Oconomowoc was that a grandpa and his grandson were horrible donation attendants. One day the cars stopped coming; it was like a light switch got turned off.

My grandpa and I sat in the donations room for 3 or 4 days with no donations. Sid came down in a panic after day 4.

He came down to bum a smoke from us and he said, "What did you guys do? There are no donations coming in! You guys need to treat the customers better. I'm afraid we're doomed!"

My grandpa just blamed it on rummage sale season. Sid argued with this. He feared my grandpa and I were being too picky. It was bad for a while, but we were the only game in town. People came back because we were the only thrift store in Oconomowoc. Sid made us promise to treat the customers better. He also made a rule that we weren't allowed to say no anymore. We then became garbage men, because we had to throw away most of what people gave us.

The Chainsaw

Someone donated the most expensive brand of chainsaw to the store. My grandpa was the one who took in the saw. Right as my grandpa brought it in, a guy poked his head in to see what was going on in donations.

The guy looked at the saw and said, "What are you going to do with that?"

My grandpa lied through his teeth, "Well, we have to have our people check it out to make sure it's safe."

My grandpa planned to take the chainsaw home, but for the next three days the guy would pop his head in and say, "Hey! How's that chainsaw coming along?"

My grandpa would say, "We haven't had the chance to test the chainsaw yet."

The guy would say, "Here's my phone number. Call me when it's tested."

The guy came in the next day and said, "Can I buy the chainsaw yet?"

My grandpa said, "Gosh, it's been busy here. We'll let you know when it's available."

The chainsaw was already at my grandpa's house. The guy figured he was lying and stormed off mad.

On the third day, the guy stopped in, and my grandpa looked at him with a grin and said, "You know what? You're just too late... I was walking out with the chainsaw, and someone grabbed it right out of my hand!"

The guy stood silent because he knew my grandpa had really just stolen the saw. My grandpa took the chainsaw home, fixed the problem with it, and it made for a fine power tool. He later gave it to my uncle.

Breaking The Bike

One day, Agnes was working at the store doing hardlines.

Agnes rode a really nice dark green Trek Bicycle to work every day. We had a bike rack in the sorting room for the volunteers. Agnes would put her bike in the rack every day.

I was angrily moving a gaylord with the pallet jack. I was moving the big box, and I was having a hard time making the turn to put the box in the back warehouse. I started getting sweaty as I entered mania. I was entering psychosis and my anger was throbbing out my soul. The box got stuck but I kept forcing it while ripping the lodged box through the entryway. Something was blocking my box from moving with the pallet jack. I did the thing anyone would do when something is stuck. I forced it through.

The next day, Agnes took me aside and informed me that I had broken the derailleur on her Trek.

She said, "I know you'll do the right thing and pay to get my bike fixed because this is absolutely ridiculous!"

I felt so bad that I used my paycheck to pay for her bike to get fixed at the Bicycle Doctor in Dousman. Sometimes I slip up with my mental illness, and that's a shame. It only takes one second for someone to not like you anymore. You could have a lifelong friendship and in one instant be enemies. I try to be by myself as much as possible. That way when I have another episode, they know it's just me being me.

Mail Order Bride

Sid had finally met a mail order bride that wanted to be with him. After striking out in Peru, he turned his attention to the Philippines. Sid was in his mid-50s at this time. He ended up meeting a woman in her mid-30s.

He came back from that trip and said, "I could live like a king out there!"

He said, "All I need is 30,000 American dollars, and I would be rich in the Philippines!"

Sid was going to drop another $10,000 to bring her to America. She needed legal papers, a doctor's visit, and traveling money. Sid was hell bent on this woman coming to live in beautiful Oconomowoc, Wisconsin!

Suddenly, the mail order bride appeared at the thrift store. Naturally, Sid got her a job at the store sorting clothes and shoes. We would throw all donated shoes into a blue bin. Once the bins were filled, someone had to match the shoes and price them, and this is what Sid chose for his new bride to do. She sorted smelly used sneakers, boots, and sandals. It was weird to see Sid with a woman around the shop. I could tell that she already had some control over him, and that she would be wearing the pants in the relationship.

The mail order bride was very small in stature, had a ton of acne on her face, and was always silent. I never really got to know her because Sid hated me. He would only let her associate with the females that worked at the thrift store.

My grandpa always said, "Her plan is to use Sid for his money, so she can send it to her family back home."

I recently found out about Sid's whereabouts after all these years.

He had always said, "If you had 30 grand, you could live like a king in the Philippines."

That is exactly what Sid did, he took some money, moved down to the Philippines, and is living out the rest of his days on the big orbiting rock we call Earth. In my opinion, I don't know who was taking advantage of who in that situation. My grandpa was right because Sid's mail order bride always got to send money home, but Sid got to eventually live like a king for once. He always just skated by in life, so it was nice to see him flourishing, even though I hate him. I always thought I got the upper hand with him because I used the store to start my own junk business, but it was Sid who had the last laugh: living large in the Philippines with his bride.

When I moved to Milwaukee years after my thrift store employment, I got a part-time gig at the Rave working concert security. The company I did security for also played rent-a-cop at local church festivals. One weekend, I was assigned to a church in South Milwaukee; Sid was there and noticed me in my rent-a-cop uniform. He took one look at me and started laughing in an evil manner.

The Junk Truck was doing good at this time, but just the sight of me in my security outfit gave him the impression that I was washed up. I let him have his giggle, because I knew that I was doing good in life. It's funny how perceptions work in people's minds. Even though I did concert security for a fun experience, I came off as a mall cop loser just by the way I was dressed.

Pizza Party

During my years at the thrift store, my mom took a part-time job doing marketing for a Wisconsin pizza chain called Rocky Rococo. The restaurant is a chain that specializes in hot and ready pan-style pizza by the slice. In 1974, the chain was founded in Madison, Wisconsin. Rocky Rococo is true Wisconsin folklore, larger than life for us here in the cheese state. Rocky Rococo himself is a brand imagery that can convey joy, like the Oscar-Meyer Weinermobile or the Budweiser Clydesdales.

Two college students came up with the idea for the restaurant: it was modeled after Chuck E. Cheese. Instead of the mascot being a mouse, it would be a larger-than-life Italian character, Rocky Rococo, who has a mustache, wears sunglasses, is fitted in a white suit, and sports a wide-brimmed hat.

Another likeness to Chuck E. Cheese is Rocky Rococo's decor, which consists of movie posters on the walls that impose Rocky into cult classic movies with pizza puns. For instance, Rocky Rococo had one parody poster entitled *The Meatrix* after the movie *The Matrix.*

They expanded too fast and ran into financial trouble. The business was later sold to a father-and-son team who were originally from Madison, but had relocated to Oconomowoc, Wisconsin. The son went to high school with comedian Chris Farley in Madison.

The new owners agreed to let the original owners keep some of the stores in the Madison statistical area as franchises, but they would ultimately change their newly acquired restaurants from a Chuck-E.-Cheese-type concept to a quick-service pizza chain.

The original owners kept their franchises as the original game concept.

The character of Rocky Rococo was played by a gentleman named James Martin Pedersen who worked at the pizza joint with the original Madison owners.

Now with only forty locations, the modern-day big business for them is that they bake the heart-shaped pizza for Valentine's Day and give you a heart-shaped mylar balloon along with it. My mom said that Valentine's Day was their biggest day of the year. Unfortunately, my mom's heart wasn't in working for Rocky Rococo.

She spent most of her time not working on Rocky Rococo work, but designing Junk Truck ads, printing off free copies of Junk Truck fliers, and posting my ads for junk removal on Craigslist.

My mom actually named my business, The Junk Truck, by posting a random ad on Craigslist. She came up with the name The Junk Truck on the fly while she was supposed to be designing ads for Rocky Rococo. She wasn't all in on the marketing job, but she needed something that paid the bills since her real estate career had slowed down.

My mom's job at Rocky's was to take very old photos of the character Rocky Rococo, and place them in a new design, so they didn't have to shoot new promos with the actor who depicted Rocky Rococo. The company didn't want to spend money on photo shoots for new posters so they paid my mom to Photoshop new ones using the old ones.

When my mother worked for Rocky Rococo corporate, she told me that the guy who portrayed Rocky Rococo charged a pretty penny to do photo shoots. The second owners didn't hire James because he was too expensive, and he was getting older. The actor who played Rocky Rococo started to not look like Rocky Rococo from his glory days of the 1980s. James Martin Pedersen would still play the character from time to time if a new movie came out that the company absolutely had to lampoon with pizza puns.

Much like the pizza chain was snatched from the original owners, I was about to do something similar, but on a smaller scale to put some Benjamins in my pocket. This was gonna be like taking candy from a baby.

My grandpa's greediness had really rubbed off on me, and I was now human garbage. I saw every opportunity to use the thrift store for financial gain. This meant even using employees to get ahead.

I had come up with quite the audacious plan to ask all the young employees and community service kids if they wanted Rocky Rococo pan pizza for lunch. I would collect everyone's money, but then use the free pizza cards my Mom gave me to pick up the pizza pies, and pocket the cash for myself! I went around to Sydney Binfield first. She was sorting clothes.

Sydney Binfield was a tall athletic-looking brunette. She was drop-dead gorgeous. You would never guess that she was a full-blown stoner. Sydney was fresh out of high school, so she had a youthful look to her. It would be easy to persuade her.

I said, "Hey, I'm feeling like getting Rocky Rococo pizza for lunch. You down to chip in?"

Sydney Binfield said, "That sounds so good, yes!"

Next, I went up to another female employee, and she loved the idea. I then approached a few others, and they said that they were excited to order Rocky's. My plan seemed to be working until I was about to place the order.

Just as sure as nobody can agree on what pizza toppings to get, everyone started to ponder aloud the idea of pizza joints to consider *other* than Rocky's. Sydney Binfield suggested we get Domino's. A community service volunteer said, "Let's get Pizza Hut!" My scheme to scam my colleagues was falling apart before my eyes.

How was I going to get my team back on track? I needed to make them order Rocky Rococo or I wouldn't be able to line my pockets with their dough. I took a page out of my grandpa's motorcycle gang playbook, and I used master manipulation to gain my advantage. We were all standing around at this point while everyone named a different pizza place we should order.

I said, "I'm not driving to get the food unless it's Rocky Rococo."

Barely anybody else drove, so they had to go with my idea. Everybody caved and I went upstairs to the break room to order the pizzas, so they wouldn't hear me mention the free pizza cards.

You had to call ahead if you were going to use multiple Rocky free pizza cards, so I made the call to let the Oconomowoc location know about my pizza party. The restaurant agreed to make multiple pizzas for free because I claimed to be from corporate.

Ten minutes later, I was on my way in my windowless maroon Toyota Corolla to grab the goods. I reached my destination, grabbed the pan-style pizzas, and placed them on my black moldy seats. I got back to the store, and everyone dug into the pizza pies.

Sydney Binfield said, "Travis, this was a good choice!"

I left work that day with date night money to take my girlfriend out to eat with. I had done something intrepid. But I didn't always use these free pizza cards for evil.

While on vacation in Wisconsin Dells, I gave a family in need a free pizza card. My mom gave my girlfriend and me a bunch of free pizza cards to use on vacation, so we could save money on food.

We kept going to the Rocky Rococo that was owned by the original owner. We were amazed at how different the Madison area restaurants were than the ones back home. The original Rocky's had an arcade where you could win prizes. We could feel the energy was off as soon as we walked in.

A bathing suit-clad family, wearing T-shirts over their suits, wet at the bottom, stood at the counter.

The mother complained to the cashier, proclaiming, "We're from Illinois, we eat here every summer in Wisconsin Dells. You can't make this right?"

The mother was appalled at the young pimple-faced cashier's customer service. The teenage cashier just shook his head in response. My girlfriend and I looked at each other with the same idea. Without haste, I approached the family with a free pizza card in hand.

I walked up to the matriarch of the family and said, "Hey there, my mom works for Rocky Rococo Corporate, and the owners would never want you to have a bad experience. This location is a franchise and has nothing to do with corporate. Here you go! Have a free pizza!"

The woman gave the free pizza card to the cashier who now was very annoyed that I just saved the day. The woman thanked my girlfriend and me as she waited for her free pan pizza. It felt good that day to make a family smile.

Years later, after my breakup with my girlfriend, I lived above a bar. At the time, I sported a mustache and a pair of sideburns. This girl

Janie used to party with us at my apartment. We were passing the bong around and she shouted, "You look like Rocky Rococo!"

I was embarrassed at the time, for she would always call me "Rocky Rococo" after that. She even told me that I should contact the restaurant about portraying Rocky Rococo for them.

A while later, I wore my Rocky Rococo look like a badge of honor. I told people at parties about how I was going to get hired as Rocky when the real actor died.

I ended up becoming old, bald, and fat before that ever happened. On February 4, 2016, James Martin Pedersen, the actor who played Rocky Rococo passed away. I never reached out to corporate to give my condolences, offer my services to portray Rocky Rococo, and steal a dead man's job. It was a missed connection to finally become the real Rocky Rococo. Rest in peace, Rocky!

Crack Break

You could argue the case for gender discrimination at the thrift store, in the sense that my grandpa would only hire men to work donations. That all changed when this curly-haired, tall, and slightly husky woman showed up. She wore JNCO Jeans and a T-shirt from a local tavern.

Kaylee was a stereotypical tomboy. She had frizzy, dark blonde curly hair. She looked like a heavyset Little Debbie. She had a face full of freckles. She had big tits that were very saggy because she never wore a bra. Her tits looked like basketballs in garbage bags. She wore clothes that resembled what the average male wore in the 1990s. She was in her early 30s.

She lived in Merton with a guy named Gary. Kaylee latched right on to my grandpa. I could tell she was attracted to him. My grandpa hired her to work in donations a few days a week.

The first day Kaylee worked, she told me that she loved smoking crack. I asked her how long she planned to live, and without blinking she said, "Until I'm 300!"

She made me laugh at how blue collar and blunt she was. We would be taking in bags of clothes, dumping them in the bin, and she would say, "Hey Travis, I'm going to take a break and go hit my crack pipe by the dumpster."

I remember thinking, "*My coworker just went on a crack break.*"

Once, I went out back by the dumpsters, and she showed me how to hit a crack pipe. The crack pipe consisted of a broken piece of hollow glass tubing. The glass pipe was filled with a Chore Boy scrubber. It only had remnants of crack rock on the Chore Boy, so

I didn't actually get high when I hit the crack pipe. She kept hitting the vapors out of the pipe while I pondered her taking my crack virginity.

Unfortunately, Kaylee's boyfriend didn't treat her right. I thought Kaylee was really sweet, but sadly she was a crackhead. She was very gullible too. You could tell her that aliens are invading and she would believe you and just might go into hiding. She is still a very good memory in my mind.

The Call Came from Inside the Store

Ethan and I were really bored one Saturday. The donations were coming in every now and then. It was me, Kaylee, and Ethan in donations that day. Ethan and I smoked marijuana by the dumpster and headed back to the donation room to wait for more cars to show up.

Being stoned, we got bored of just sitting around, so Ethan picked up the phone, in the other room, and called us in donations. He started talking really ghetto on the phone with me, and I started playing along.

I set the phone down and said to Kaylee, "I'm in a bad way because I didn't pay my drug dealer and now he's fucking after me."

Kaylee said, "If that drug dealer calls back, I'll set him straight."

Of course, Ethan overheard this so he redialed the store with the phone by the baler. Kaylee answered this time as Ethan talked even more ghetto, claiming that he was coming to donations to kill me.

Ethan kept saying, "Bitch better have my money."

Kaylee would just try to talk the murderous drug dealer down, but he wasn't having it.

A crowd of workers and volunteers that were in on the joke was forming around Kaylee. My friend Sydney Binfield was folding clothes nearby and crying from laughter.

You could actually hear Elliot in the back room from where we were. Kaylee didn't pick up on that, so we heightened it even more.

Next, Elliot called and said, "I'm gonna shoot up the place. Where is my money at?"

Tears welled up in Kaylee's eyes and she said, "I'm scared, Travis. This isn't funny. I gotta get outta here!"

Sydney and the crowd of onlookers were laughing, but Kaylee was crying. She was probably scared because she was a crackhead who probably had dealt with real-life situations like this.

I walked back by Ethan and said, "Call back and say we're all good now. Tell her we are squared up. Kaylee is scared and that isn't right."

Ethan called back and made good with Kaylee. She said in a happy voice, "You're all good, Travis! I worked your drug debt out with them," as she patted me on the back.

The Limo

I was mastering thrift store work, I got to learn the trade from my grandpa. I had been stuffing the clothes in the baler, tied the bale up, and put the brick of clothes away with the forklift. A lot of the tasks were done for the day, but my grandpa and Kaylee were nowhere to be found. I looked in the electronics department but couldn't find them. I looked in the break room; nope, not there. The last place to check was the dumpster, so I headed that way. I saw Kaylee by electronics walking fast towards the donation area.

Kaylee was all sweaty too. I said, "Kaylee, have you seen my grandpa?"

She picked up speed and said, "NO! Sorry, Travis, haven't seen him. Have a great weekend though!"

The door to the dumpsters was a huge old steel door. It kinda looked like the steel door that Leatherface slides open to kill his victims in the Texas Chainsaw Massacre.

My grandpa drove a limo to work every day. He would park it out by the dumpster, so he could load the limo with goodies. I thought he might have been doing a heist in his limo. I was horrified at the sight I saw. I saw my grandpa, vaguely through the tinted windows of the limo, pulling up his pants and messing with his suspenders.

I screamed, "Grandpa! What the fuck are you doing?"

My grandpa put his straw hat on, opened the door, and said, "Can't a guy get a blow job around here?"

I was stunned for the rest of the day. It was a free-for-all at the thrift store in my grandpa's eyes. I didn't tell my family for a long time, but I eventually told his kids (my mom and aunt). When I told my mother about the limo incident, she was so pissed off. My mother wanted me to quit the thrift store to get away from my grandpa, but I wanted to ride this shit show out to the very end. My family still laughs about it behind my grandpa's back.

I told my girlfriend Brittany about my grandpa getting head in his limo at the thrift store. She thought it was hilarious, so she told her mom. When Brittany's mom was told about my grandpa getting head, she started to cry.

She told Brittany, "Travis doesn't stand a chance in this world."

The Jewel Heist

A patron drove in with a shiny black truck carrying a white cabinet mirror in the back to be donated. When we lifted the mirror off the truck and set it on the ground we cracked the mirror. The guy donated these white boxes that usually held jewelry. My grandpa quickly tucked them away in the mess that sat on the shelves. We then set the mirror inside, opened it up, and saw sparkling real jewelry inside. My grandpa immediately shut the cabinet.

He turned to me and said, “We have to get this into my truck, Travis!”

Just as he said that, Stacy waddled into the donation room. She walked right up to the mirror and tried to open it.

My grandpa said, “Don’t open that! It has a crack in the mirror. If you open it, the mirror might shatter!”

Stacy pulled her hand away, and said, “Let me know when this gets fixed! I want to see if there’s jewelry inside!”

My grandpa took it home, and his wife looked up the jewelry online. It was all jewelry from the Joan Rivers Collection. My grandpa spent the next few months selling the jewelry on eBay. He got so spooked that the jewelry was planted by a church member that he loaded the cabinet up with shit costume jewelry that he stole from the store. He brought the mirror back and gave it to the jewelry lady Babs, who also stole stuff. My grandpa still to this day gloats about that jewelry heist.

The Ozzman Cometh!

One day, I was working with Chaz and he said, "I just went to Fox Music in Watertown, and they have a copy of Ozzy Osbourne's *Diary of a Madman* on vinyl for sale."

I had just set up a record player in my room and needed my first record to play. All my life I was a diehard Ozzy fan. In middle school, I would write Ozzy on my knuckles just like Ozzy had on his. I told Chaz I was headed there after work. After my shift, I raced to Watertown. I parked the Corolla and ran inside, afraid that someone may have already bought it.

A kid was behind the counter, and I blurted out in a sweat, "Where is the Ozzy record?"

He didn't understand my jargon, so I repeated myself. The kid pointed behind me. I turned around and there it was! *Diary of a Madman* on vinyl! I bought it and went home to listen to it. A few months later I actually got it signed by Ozzy himself.

Before the birth of my children, if you were to ask me what the best day on earth was for me, I would say meeting Ozzy Osbourne with my mom.

One day out of the blue, my mom called me at the thrift store and said, "I just heard on the radio that Ozzy is signing autographs at a Barnes and Noble in Skokie, Illinois on January 30th. Travis, we have to go!"

This would be cool because a year or two earlier I had shelled out a ton of money to take my mom to see Ozzy and Rob Zombie in Milwaukee, at the Bradley Center. We called Barnes and Noble and they were grumpy about answering questions concerning Ozzy's appearance.

Some old bitch said, in a cold tone, "Ozzy is only signing copies of his new book, *I Am Ozzy...*"

I was bummed because I wanted Ozzy to sign my *Diary of a Madman* album. The day to meet the Ozz man himself finally came. My mom and I were fighting like usual about meaningless shit.

I said, "Fuck it! I'm not bringing my *Diary of a Madman* album."

My mom encouraged me to bring it just in case. I ran down to my room in the basement, grabbed the album, took off the protective sleeve, and ran out the door. I took off work at the thrift store on that Saturday so I could be there when the Ozzman cometh.

My mom and I fought all the way from Oconomowoc, Wisconsin to Skokie, Illinois with times in between when we told each other to, "Chill out!"

As we passed through the Illinois tolls, my mom and I started to have fun listening to songs on her 6 CD changer under the seat in her gold Acura MDX. We left home at 5 in the morning to get to the mall by 7 when the parking lot opened to the Old Orchard Mall. People were just driving around circling the parking lot like vultures waiting for the lot to open. I left my *Diary of a Madman* album in the car because they specifically said Ozzy wouldn't sign the album.

It was a little after 7:00 a.m. by the time we got to the mall and there were already 400 people waiting in line to meet Ozzy. My heart sank to also notice that this was an outdoor mall, so we would be standing outside in the freezing January cold. Ozzy was going to be there at 1 PM, so from 7 AM to 1 PM we would become ice cubes. My mom and I got in line to just literally chill. Everyone in line was a huge Ozzy fan which made the time pass. My mom and I befriended a younger mom who had a son in middle school. We all talked about Ozzy in such a magical way.

This creepy guy kept trying to cut everyone in line. He looked like a little troll who drank too much booze, smoked too many cigarettes, and beat his meat to *Hustler*. My mom was disgusted by this short man.

She said, "I'm pissed that this guy thinks he can cut the line when we have stood here since the mall opened. I'm doing something about this bullshit!"

My mom ratted him out to the bookstore employees, and he got thrown to the back of the line. There may have been vulgar words exchanged by the guy.

About two hours into leaning against a cold concrete wall, a bookstore employee came out and said that Ozzy had informed them that he could only stay for two hours once he arrived.

I turned to my mom and said, "We aren't even going to meet Ozzy now."

With that, my mom became a wicked monster, and said, "Fuck this, Travis I'm tired of standing out here in the cold."

The problem was that the bookstore was already at capacity so we *had* to suffer in the cold.

My mom marched up to the book seller and said, "Can I go inside and buy Ozzy's book for him to sign?"

The guy nodded yes and my mom said, "Go grab that mother and son we were talking to and let's go cut the line."

With that, I grabbed them and we headed inside to be warm. We jumped the line by about 250 people. I laughed inside because my mom had made that other guy go to the back of the line. We sat on the floor in the store and talked to the mother and son about life and rock music. We learned they were from Peoria and the mother had pulled the boy out of school to meet Ozzy. I ended up seeing Alex Stafford who is the Metal DJ of Milwaukee. I met Alex at my first Gwar show. He was trying to fish a twinkly out of his pocket and I thought he was pickpocketing me while we waited for the almighty Gwar to take the stage. I talked to him about the Milwaukee scene for a while and then I returned to hang with my mom, the other mom, and the kid. We sat for another hour or so and then suddenly a silver tour bus was driving by the store's big bay windows. We all got up and started to get ready to meet the Prince of Darkness.

As the line moved, they played Ozzy music over the loudspeaker. Songs like, "Waiting for Darkness" and "Rock 'n' Roll Rebel" played over the store's stereo. A kid walked out with a Black Sabbath vinyl autographed.

I turned to my mom and said, "Fuck! We left my *Diary of a Madman* in the car!"

My mom turned around and said, "I'm running to the car to get it!"

I said, "You'll never make it in time!"

We were only a few people away from seeing Ozzy. She turned around and ran so fast. My mom is a smoker, and I didn't know she could run like that. I was freaking out because we were getting close to meeting Ozzy, and my mom still wasn't back. My mom then appeared running down the aisles of the bookstore. She huffed and puffed with the album in hand. The line of people was moving forward and we were about to meet the Blizzard of Ozz.

Ozzy was tucked away signing autographs in the CD room of Barnes and Noble. The area had a light yellow tagboard that held up the shelves for the compact discs. To the right of Ozzy was a huge standup banner of the cover of Ozzy's new book, *I Am Ozzy*. To the left of that banner was another banner made specifically by Barnes and Noble. The banner read, "Barnes and Noble- Ozzy Osbourne-Saturday, January 30th, 2010."

I could see Ozzy Osbourne now! Ozzy was dressed in all black wearing a silver cross around his neck. Ozzy was also sporting his famous purple circular glasses. He was heavily guarded by grumpy booksellers who kept walking the aisles looking for Ozzy contraband. Ozzy's personal assistant, Tony Dennis, stood glaring at all of us like a gargoyle. Ozzy's personal assistant has appeared numerous times on the MTV Show *The Osbournes.* Tony Dennis was always by Ozzy's side in any public appearances. He was dressed in a blue and gray flannel. He stood with his arms behind his back, expressionless, and just watched Ozzy sign books.

Next to Ozzy's personal assistant was a big fat security guard who was dressed in an all-black suit. The security guard had gray hair and wore glasses. He just peered over Ozzy's shoulder. Next to the security guard was one of Skokie's finest. On the right side stood a husky, bald police officer with his hands at his side. They kept shouting, "Ozzy will only sign the book!" I kept the *Diary of a Madman* vinyl behind my back. Ozzy was in sight now!

They were so protective of Ozzy that you couldn't hand him the book yourself to sign. You had to hand the book directly to a Barnes and Noble staff member, and they would hand it to Ozzy. My mom was about to hand the book to the staff member who looked straight out of the 1980s. The staff member was a short, old brunette woman with glasses. She wore a very dated 1980's women's blue business suit equipped with shoulder pads. She was a real bitch too.

Right as my mom handed the book to the seller, I revealed the vinyl and said, "Ozzy, would you sign this?"

Ozzy is awesome to his fans because he replied, "Absolutely!"

In typical Ozzy fashion, he did not give a fuck about the signing-only-the-book rule! I handed the album to Shoulder Pads and Ozzy signed it. My mom snapped a photo of me throwing the horns up while Ozzy was looking down. My friend Alex Stafford had the same photo opp with Ozzy; Alex throwing the horns up, and Ozzy looking down!

My mom told Ozzy, "You smell very nice, Ozzy!"

I told him something dorky like, "Ozzy, you're my favorite artist."

He has probably heard that one a million times.

In the words of Chris Farley, "Idiot!"

That was it for meeting him. The staff member in a lavender sweater gave me an evil look as she handed me my signed album. My mom and I ran out on an adrenaline rush. We got in line at 6 AM and Ozzy didn't start signing until around 2 PM. Meeting Ozzy lasted all of fifty seconds, but it was worth waiting around all day. We exited through the CD section of the store.

As I passed by music listening stations for the CD's, a kid said to us, "Damnit, Ozzy is signing albums!"

Before my mom's alcoholism took over, I was lucky to have a mom like mine because she never let me give up on getting that vinyl signed. My mom and I haven't really had a relationship in a long time, but it is nice to have a memory like that to cherish. As we left that day laughing, there was a line around the whole mall to meet Ozzy. I heard afterwards that there were 1,000 people waiting to meet Ozzy that day, but the only person I wanted to be with was my mom.

Donation Of The Damned

We would get high by the dumpsters all the time now when management wasn't at the thrift store. Sydney Binfield and I were getting high in the back, complaining about work.

I started bitching, "I can't take this shit anymore. They have me working my ass off for no fucking money."

I took a hit from the pipe and handed it to Sydney Binfield. I blew out the hit and started to cough. Sydney took a hit from the pipe, held it in, and started to bitch as she exhaled.

She complained, "This place has us overworked. I'm about to quit. This is such bullshit!"

Sydney's friend Brea was like, "Look what you guys are doing! You're getting high at work and barely working! Don't take this for granted!"

It's crazy how correct Brea was. We were in the best years of our lives, and we didn't recognize it. Being young is truly wasted on the youth... We got back to donations feeling buzzed, and ready to take on the workload.

I was in charge of donations on Saturdays, but my pay didn't reflect that. We would get a fair amount of donations that I didn't get paid enough to put up with. We had a sister thrift store in nearby Waukesha. That store had a truck that would do pickups like Purple Heart does. The truck would pick up nothing but junk. We would unload a whole box truck full of clothes in black garbage bags. When we would dump the clothes out of the black bags, dirty diapers would be mixed in with the clothes.

Another weird donation that I received on a Saturday came on a busy day. Cars were pulling up fast and dropping off furniture, clothes, and hard goods. People were filling out their tax slips and the donation area was packed with couches and desks that were donated. There was a line of customers waiting to tear off a donation tax slip.

A woman came in with a weird look on her face. It was a wicked smirk. She was in a flowered dress and handed me a box and bolted out. I was with some high school boys who were doing community service. We opened the box and it was filled with dildos, vibrators, and other various sex toys. Why would a woman think that a religious thrift store could use a fake dick that had been up her twat? I was stunned with no words, but I was also plagued with curiosity. Unraveling that is like knowing how many licks it takes to get to the center of a Tootsie Pop. The world may never know.

The Dresser

I have slept on the floor since the third grade. I would just lay on a nest of blankets. I would leave my clothes on the floor and didn't have a dresser. Now that I was in my early 20s, my mom wanted me to get a dresser. She wanted me to find direction and be an adult. Organizing my clothes might be the big step I needed!

I worked at a thrift store, so I knew furniture. I wanted a cream-of-the-crop dresser. I wanted my clothes to sit in royal splendor. On a dreary day, my grandpa and I were outside smoking cigarettes. My prayer was answered in the form of a box truck that read "Furniture Store." Two guys jumped out of the cab. One had a clipboard in his hand.

The Clipboard Guy asked, "Who's the manager?"

My grandpa motioned that he was and took the clipboard.

The guy said, "Our bosses just want to know that we didn't steal this dresser for ourselves."

My grandpa signed a form saying that he received the dresser. The men then unloaded a brand-new dresser. It had pillars of woodwork with wooden vines running up the sides. The dresser that my grandpa and I were going to steal was made out of gorgeous cherrywood. It was a brand new artisan dresser. The delivery men told us that someone returned it to their store, so they wanted to donate the dresser to us!

We got it inside donations with a dolly, and I was running around with anxiety.

"Grandpa, I *need* this dresser. Let's load it up before anyone sees it."

"It's too risky, Travis. We should wait two weeks. I'll put 500 dollars on it so no one buys it until we can lift it."

Just then doodly Sid came in and oohed and ahhed at it.

He said, "This is a breathtaking piece." Like he fucking knew anything about furniture.

Sid liked to pretend that he was on the up-and-up with thrift store prices.

He asked, "How much are you going to put on this dresser?"

My grandpa smiled and said, "500 bucks."

Sid instantly said, "It's worth every penny. Do it!"

With the OK to price it so high no one would ever buy it, we would be lined up to steal it.

Two weeks went by and the dresser sat priced at 500 bucks. Towards the end of work on a Friday afternoon, my grandpa was about to leave. He walked away, paused in place, and turned to me.

He said, "Today is the day. Go get the flat cart from the warehouse!"

I ran to the back, retrieved the dolly, and we laid the dresser on its back on the cart. My grandpa and I weaved the cart through the aisles where no one saw us with the dresser. We used the clothes racks as cover as we went through the circled-window grocery doors.

My grandpa had a white van parked by the dumpster. We opened the doors and tried to shove the dresser in the back of the van. There was too much stolen shit from the thrift store inside. We were stuck with the dresser in midair for anyone to catch us red-handed.

My grandpa looked at me and said, "Make a really big push. Shove this fucker in there!"

With all our might we jammed the dresser just in there enough to close the doors. My grandpa and I were shaking because of how fucking insane that was. We could have been caught at any moment! My grandpa got out of Dodge and I jumped in my car to meet him at my mom's house. I was eager to tell her that I found a dresser! Years later, the dresser looked ratty, so I donated it to the same brand thrift store that was near me in Milwaukee. Eventually they got the dresser back! Dents, scratches and all! So technically I only borrowed it for a while.

The Shopping Spree

When I dropped out of high school, all of my friends graduated and moved to Milwaukee. They all got to experience the college daze while I stayed back in our hometown. Oconomowoc being a 45-minute drive to the big city made it hard to see them. One of the many Saturdays that I was at the store playing manager, my friend Brian called me there. He wanted to come to see me in action at work.

I bluntly said, "If you come down here, bring your mom's van because I am giving you a free shopping spree! Anything that fits in your mom's van is free!" He was shocked!

He said, "I'll be there in a few."

I found Brian walking the aisles a few minutes later. I was angry about being at work, so I just walked around with him. The store would price portable Walkmans super high, even though the public was living in an iPod era. The stuff would just sit in bins on the shelf because the volunteers had the prices jacked.

Brian said, "Can I have a Walkman?"

I laughed and handed him the whole box of 40 Walkmans and said, "Take the whole fucking box! I'm sick of this shit!"

I took the box for Brian to be whisked out the door later. (Brian later used the box of Walkmans to teach himself how to circuit-bend electronics.) Next, I brought Brian into the sorting room. Harry Peter had built these wire cages that housed instruments to be appraised. The problem was that the music stuff just collected dust. The volunteers thought they had Ringo Starr's snare drum when in reality it was all just old instruments.

I said, "Fuck this shit; take these fucking instruments that these idiots won't price."

I was such an asshole! I let Brian take a snare drum, trumpet, and trombone. I closed the wire cages and set the instruments with the Walkmans. Brian picked out knickknacks and odd finds throughout the old thrift store.

We usually snuck stuff out of donations, but I made Brian drive by the dumpster to pick up his goodies. I opened the old steel door by the compactor and Brian gasped.

He said, "Shit, I thought I was caught for sure."

I laughed, "No, just me! Let me help you load this stuff in your mom's van."

We loaded the stolen loot, hugged, and he drove off to the big city to forget about me again.

That Monday, Sid came stomping in and asked, "What happened Saturday?"

I played dumb, but he questioned me about all the missing items.

I said, "We had some unruly high-school volunteers this weekend. I bet one of those punks took that stuff!"

Sid bought the story. He believed anything my grandpa and I would lie to him about. He just took my word for it. Funny little man.

The Ship Room

Towards the end of my tenure with the thrift store, my grandpa had really turned the store around. When Buck was the donations manager, the store looked like a pigsty. My grandpa organized the store to be neat and orderly. He would write funny quotes on the price tags as if the furniture was human and could speak to you. "I'm tall, dark, and handsome! I would look great in your bedroom!" on a dresser. People loved walking the furniture aisles to see what the furniture would say next. It was comedy gold!

His whole life, my grandpa built model ships and admired lighthouses. He turned the donation area into the captain's quarters of a ship. He had lighthouse statues all over the room. He had a picture of a ship above the doors that led into the sorting room. He had knickknack figurines of ship captains around the room. We were ass-backwards stealing stuff, but the store was a well-oiled machine now. I was still being an asshole to the customers because I was burnt out. My grandpa was an asshole to the customers *and* his employees, because it was second nature to him.

My grandpa fired everyone he hired. One guy came in wanting hours, so we hired him. This new recruit was supposed to work on Saturday with me, but he never showed. That Monday the new recruit showed up for work like nothing happened.

"Where were you on Saturday?" my grandpa demanded.

"I am so sorry. My grandma died and her funeral was Saturday. I'll be there this next weekend for sure."

The next Saturday came and went with the new recruit pulling another no-call no-show. That Monday the new recruit showed his face again, like nothing had happened.

My grandpa met the guy by his car and shouted at him, "What, did your grandma die again? You're fired, you piece of shit!"

We never saw that employee again. The only employee that didn't ever get fired was Brandon Evans.

The thrift store management was starting to turn on us. They never believed in me. When I launched my junk removal business, my stepdad bought me professional signs for my truck. I started driving the truck to the thrift store to park it by the road, for advertising purposes. I think I got away with it one shift before Sid came running in donations to complain.

He came in and bitched at my grandpa, "Travis can't park his truck like that!"

My grandpa was like, "Why? He's just parking his truck." I don't remember Sid's answer, but deep down I knew why. Sid didn't want me to succeed because he hated my guts. Sid and Harry Peter had a fit about the Junk Truck being in front at the thrift store because they were fucking bitches who didn't want to support me.

The way Sid acted reminded me of when he gave everyone in the store a 50-cent raise and me a 10-cent raise. When he and Harry Peter treated me as less than human, it made me giggle about robbing the store blind. They were out to get me, but I was laughing all the way to the bank! They should have supported my new junk removal business, but like always, they treated me like a turd that was dangling from a homeless bum's anus! They treated me like the minimum wage slave that I was.

In retaliation, I started using the thrift store as my personal dump for The Junk Truck. I would drive my truck to work, and I'd unload the truck into the compactor when they weren't looking. I loaded up a bunch of junk in Brookfield, then I drove it right to the thrift store. As I backed up the Junk Truck, my grandpa started yelling. He thought I was insane.

He shouted, "We're going to get caught throwing junk into the compactor! Sid is still in the store, Travis!"

I had Baby Huey and my grandpa unload the truck, then pulled out of the parking lot a few hundred dollars richer from the pickup job and not having to pay to dump it.

Another day, I loaded some lumber into the compactor that got lodged in the mouth of the dumpster. Stacy came out and took one look at all the lumber.

"Where did this come from? We don't take building materials."

I just replied, "Someone dumped that wood on us when we weren't looking!

She didn't buy it! But my junk removal business was taking off now. Slowly, I had passed enough fliers out to subdivisions that business started picking up. First, I slashed the hours that I would take donations to only a few days a week. Now, I was starting to be able to live off junk removal. It made me proud that I had a crazy idea of being a full-time junk man, and I had seen the idea through into a full-fledged business. I finally had the confidence that I didn't have in high school or by working my dead-end job at the thrift store. In high school, I told my guidance counselor that I was going to be a bum, and when I started taking pots and pans home from the thrift store, I wanted to be just like Luis and his bum employee. In the end, I had turned corporate though. I was no longer the bum because The Junk Truck went from a scrappy kid with a truck picking up metal for free to a real business that held liability insurance and charged for pickups. Instead of looking up to the bums, I now looked up to Brian Scudamore, the owner of the very successful "1-800-Got-Junk?" I fought "the man" all my life but I had morphed into the man as I looked in the mirror today.

Sid told my grandpa, "Now that Travis's junk business is going well, I think we should part ways with him." That was how I faded out of employment with the thrift store. Even though I wasn't an employee anymore, I would still stop by on a Saturday, to smoke some bud when there was no management there. I would show up on Saturday, meet Sydney by the compactor, and smoke with her. On one sunny Saturday afternoon, Sydney and I were smoking weed when the metal door swung open. Harry Peter stormed out with steam coming from his ears.

He pointed at me and said, "You don't work here! Get out!"

I shuffled off in a panic back to my Corolla. I would say that was the last time that I messed up at the thrift store, but something sinister was brewing in my mind. The Geier gears of crime were turning...

Before I quit the thrift store, I stole one of the keys to the compactor. My thought was that I had used and abused every aspect of the thrift store, so why stop now? I discovered how expensive it is to dump a truckload of junk at our local landfill, so I would use the thrift store as my own personal landfill.

After I quit, I would only use the compactor on Sundays when the store was closed for a day of religious observation. I would load my truck full of junk for a customer on a Saturday, and I would unload the crap into the store's compactor on a Sunday. The key I stole would work the ram to push all the junk into the container for pick up. The ram was really loud when it was pulverizing the trash, so I was concerned about neighbors' complaints.

There was only one house that could see me in the back of the store, and I prayed that they would never spill the beans. Eventually, the neighbors became concerned that someone was

pulling in the back of the store after hours. Someone ratted me out, and my phone rang off the hook that day.

I answered. A very mad Harry Peter greeted me on the other end, screaming, "YOU ARE NEVER ALLOWED TO BE ON OUR PROPERTY AGAIN! WE FOUND OUT THAT YOU HAVE BEEN USING THE COMPACTOR! DON'T EVER SHOW YOUR FACE HERE AGAIN!" CLICK! That was the end of the free landfill for The Junk Truck. It also marked me not being allowed to step foot on the thrift store's property ever again.

I feel bad about using the compactor for my own personal business. It was extremely wrong, and I also question why I acted the way I did when I worked there. Why did I treat the store, employees, and customers like crap? It is because I was out of my mind at the time. By doing all that destructive behavior, I was fueling my manic episodes. It felt good to take, take, take. Now, I paid for it though, because I know deep down that I am a horrible person and I have to live with what I've done. My time at the thrift store was over for good. After I quit the store, my grandpa worked six more months as the donations manager. Right before I left my job at the thrift store, this guy from the Philippines got hired at the thrift store.

At first, my grandpa really liked this guy because he used to be an in-home caretaker for the disabled and elderly. My grandpa told me tales of this guy's battle in the trenches of in-home care.

My grandpa said, "The new guy said that he would have to put a rubber glove on and stick his hand up an old guy's ass to get the impacted poop to make his bowels drop."

That really made me laugh thinking of a guy with his hand up an old man's ass to make him take a shit, but something was off with this guy. The thrift store started to feel like an episode of Game of Thrones now.

Right before I quit, I remember my grandpa saying, "I don't trust this guy, Travis. Let's not steal in front of him."

An influx of new employees were getting hired now, and it was really changing the workplace culture. The guy from the Philippines wanted my grandpa's job. All he had to do was just squeeze my grandpa out inch by inch. The Filipino would eventually get his way.

The problem was that my grandpa was still up to his old tricks; even though I was long gone. A man inquired about wanting to donate a car to the thrift store. My grandpa wanted to steal the car. My grandpa told the guy that he would come look at the car on his day off to see if the store would be interested.

He stopped out and the guy had a beautiful Lincoln Town Car that he wanted to donate to the store. After talking to the gentlemen, my grandpa discovered that this guy just retired from the FBI! My grandpa was in a pinch! My grandpa thought of every angle. He even ran the heist by a brother in his motorcycle gang.

The second that my grandpa mentioned that the donation was from a retired FBI agent, the brother turned around and ignored him the rest of the night. My grandpa knew he couldn't do it. He ended up declining the offer to have the store accept the car.

The board of directors were starting to become leery of my grandpa's management skills. They suspected my grandpa of stealing. My grandpa was stealing metal one day. He was caught by Harry Peter mid-dump of the metal into the back of his pickup truck. When questioned about it by Harry Peter, my grandpa said, "I'm donating the metal to a 12-step program."

Harry Peter didn't believe it for a second. One day Harry Peter showed up to give grandpa his notice. He patted my grandpa on the shoulder and said, "Your services are no longer needed here."

The captain was kicked off of his pirate ship! I didn't think much of what would become of the ship room because I was so busy with junk removal now. Brandon Evans still worked at the thrift store. He told me that the guy from the Philippines got the job as the new donations manager. Brandon informed me that the first thing he did was get rid of everything ship-related that my grandpa had decorated the donations room with. With that, my grandpa and I were erased from the thrift store. He really did turn out to be a wolf in sheep's clothing after all. I ran into the Filipino guy like six months later, and he acted all buddy, buddy with me, like he didn't steal my grandpa's job, rat us out, and act like his shit didn't stink. Brandon Evans moved to Milwaukee. He invited me to a big party he was having. I drove to Milwaukee to smoke some buds with my Oconomowoc buddies who lived in the Brew City now. As I blew out a hit of weed, I saw the ship painting that had hung in donations. It was on the wall at Brandon's new apartment.

I looked at Brandon and said, "Give me my grandpa's fucking painting! That painting symbolizes my time working with him."

Brandon shook his head and said, "You can have it for 30 bucks."

I blurted out, "Fuck no! That is my grandpa's painting! Give it to me right fucking now!"

I went home empty-handed that night. I fought with Brandon about the painting at three of his parties until I shelled out the dough.

At the fourth party, I stormed up to Brandon's apartment, and said, "Here is 30 bucks, bastard. Now get my painting down!"

Brandon took the painting down and I went to put it in my truck during the party. I finally had a piece of the wreckage from what was left of the ship room. As I hung the painting on the wall of my apartment I thought, "The port was finally closed. The lighthouse was burned out once and for all."

Epilogue

After my time at the thrift store ended, I tweaked a famous saying to make sense of my tenure of employment. My version goes, "Christianity ends in the parking lot of the Catholic thrift store." In the thrift business, there was definitely a disconnect between Sunday worship and Monday through Saturday life. In the Bible, the Book of James states "Faith by itself, if it is not accompanied by action, is dead." - James 2:17. I wonder what James would have thought of our actions being so closely associated with the church. I wonder what he would have thought of how we were treated by our higher-ups.

I worked at the thrift store for three and a half years. The whole experience felt like a bad after-school special. The description of the episode on the preview channel would have read,

"After eighteen-year-old Travis Geier leads police on a painfully slow car chase, he is tasked with straightening out his young life. Travis finds himself working at a Catholic thrift store in his hometown of Oconomowoc, Wisconsin. At work, he has an inkling that all isn't what it seems at his new place of employment. Travis discovers that all of the employees are stealing donations from the thrift store. Soon, Travis gets his motorcycle-gang-member grandpa a job as the donations manager. Together, Travis and his grandpa start a series of money schemes that make them legends in their own minds. The gangster biker and his young grandson must navigate the criminal underworld of the Catholic thrift store. Along the way, they coexist with colleagues who are thieves, sex addicts, and crackheads. This is the true story of a grandpa and grandson turning trash into treasure."

When the after-school special goes to commercial break, there would be a public service announcement starring a kid that once volunteered at the thrift store. He's bartending with Eve years later, and he tells her, "Working at the thrift store was so messed up because they were all crackheads there." Sadly, the public service announcement was a real-life conversation that Eve had working with this volunteer. I personally think the volunteer was wrong about us. There was beauty in our dead souls. To me, all the best, most creative employees were rogues.

My grandpa and I banded together because we were thick as thieves. The core group of workers also never snitched on each other, for we were all fighting against the grain of the evil force that was the board of directors. We were mice looking for cheese, and the board was the mouse trap ready to snap on us. I truly believe that the saying, "there's no honor among thieves" isn't true because of how we as employees had our heads dunked in the toilet for so long. The swirlie we received by the board of directors was a fun carnival ride because it made us stronger as people. I interviewed Emily while writing this book, and she said something that struck me. "Travis, when we worked at the thrift store together, you always said that my sister Eve was so old. Travis, we were in our twenties, and I didn't realize it at the moment, but working at the thrift store was the best time of our lives." That blew my mind while listening back to our recording because it really was such a special time. We just didn't know it yet. My grandpa was a lot younger then and I was drinking from the fountain of youth when we were working together. The weed wasn't fucking with me yet either. Girls found me attractive, not fat and bald. The thrift store was a job where we could slack off. A job where I could build my business The Junk Truck on the side. I got to tell the craziest stories to entertain people at parties. I have a plethora of memories with my grandpa, both good and bad.

I waited a decade before returning to the thrift store. I only went now and then with my girl, but when I wrote this book, I went a few times in one week. I wanted to jog my memory about what had all taken place. A lot had changed about the store. I walked back by the bathrooms and saw Bugs shifting through the clothes.

I laughed to myself and said, "This place looks different, but some things never change."

Bugs looked slim and healthy as he looked through the clothes.

Part of me wanted to say hi, but I decided against it because I thought he might look mysterious and say, "You shouldn't be here."

When I returned home, I sat on my favorite chair, the one made out of a stump, and I gazed upon the ship painting. As I looked at the work of art, I thought back fondly on my time working with my grandpa. My favorite part of working at the thrift store was how it brought our family together. My best memory of my time there was one year approaching the Geier Christmas Gathering. My grandpa had made a rule that everyone in the family had to give each other Christmas presents from a thrift store. My grandpa ended up stealing everybody a present from the store; we all complied and had gifts for each other. After we opened our gifts, my grandpa and I told our family stories of all the ways customers would try to donate broken stuff to us.

I remember laughing so hard that my cheeks and belly hurt. My family laughed as we told the next way a customer would try to justify giving us piss-stained blankets or broken speakers. That's one of my favorite memories from my time working at the thrift store, because it reminds me of when everyone in my family got along. It's sad that everyone in my family is at war with each other now.

When I look at the ship painting, it can be a double-edged sword. It makes me feel remorse and sorrow as much as I feel happy. A lot of my memories of working at the thrift store are also bittersweet. For every happy memory of the place, there is a memory of it that is tainted by our workplace dysfunction. The moral of the story is, "Don't slack off because you'll become a weed smoker who works at a criminal thrift store, and eventually becomes a junk man."

The ship painting reminds me of the weird way my grandpa showed us love as kids. The painting reminds me of how much I love my grandpa for who he is. My grandpa was a bad guy, but he was always there for me. He may have shown me a swastika when I was 5 years old, but he was always there to pick me up for hockey practice. My grandpa was always there to take me to a monster truck rally as a kid, but he glorified being the bad guy too. The old man is a very twisted person, but he has always looked out for me. People always ask me why I still talk to my grandpa. The answer is that I look at his actions toward me, and not at the man. My grandfather is a psychopath, but he's my psychopath.

Lastly, the ship painting signifies that I got to have a relationship with my grandfather. Some people never get to meet their grandfather. Who can say their grandpa was their manager, and it wasn't even a family business. It was for a chain of thrift stores that never believed in me, but my grandpa always did. After our time working together, we sailed off into other ventures in life. I started a junk removal company called The Junk Truck which I later turned into a book of the same name. As for my grandpa, he officially retired and now farts around his house and yard full of treasures he's collected during his life. He's taking it easy for once. He finally didn't need to fake disability or workman's comp anymore, because he is on a long-term sabbatical now.

He is really enjoying life! It's fun to watch my grandfather in the twilight of his life. Whenever I am with him, I want to remember my grandpa as a family man.

My grandpa has always been there to guide my family through life's toughest challenges. He always helped me sail through the deep tides of life. He helped me tread water through the giant waves of grief I was feeling. He always knows what wisdom to spew. Whenever anything goes wrong in my life, my grandpa will always say, "Fuck 'em, Travis!" And he's right... fuck 'em!

My grandfather and I weren't just the donations manager and donations attendant. We were radical pirates of a ghost pirate ship. My grandfather was the sleazy captain of the ship, and I was his first mate. Our choices at work were selfish, wrong, and downright evil. We failed to help others, but we helped ourselves. We were the Thrift Store Mafia!

THE END.

A young Travis Geier in the 2000s, working at the thrift store.

Acknowledgments

First off, I would like to thank the five people I interviewed for this book. They wanted to remain anonymous, but this book wouldn't have been possible without their contributions. Next, I would like to thank my team who contributed to this book: Caylee Wells, Ann Klefstad, Emma Geier, Stacy Odell, and Brandon Evans. I would like to tell both my sons that I love them so much. You boys are my biggest inspiration to be a better human being. Dad loves you both very much. I would also like to tell my retired racing greyhound Fiction that I love him, too. Thank you for showing me unconditional love, Fiction. A big nod goes out to my retired racing greyhounds that crossed over the Rainbow Bridge, Willow Run Chalk and N.B's Sugarcat. I miss you silly hounds. I want to give a big thank you to my grandfather for always believing in me whether it is doing junk removal, improv comedy, or writing. I love you grandpa. I would like to thank Dave Odell. I would like to give a thanks to Nick Wesell for always standing by me as a friend. Lastly, I would love to thank people in my life that have passed on from this world. Thank you to my Grandma Mimi, Trevor Adonis, and Corey Nowak. I never stop thinking about you three. You are my biggest inspiration to keep going in life. Thank you for the memories that we shared together.

About The Author

Travis Geier is the author of Thrift Store Mafia and The Junk Truck. He resides with his family in Milwaukee, Wisconsin. Travis' best friend is his retired racing Greyhound, Fiction. He is an avid fan of Garfield the Cat and horror movies. Travis previously performed long-form improv comedy, and scare acted in haunted houses for 7 years. Travis is a recovered addict who carries the message of sobriety.

www.ingramcontent.com/pod-product-compliance
Lightning Source LLC
LaVergne TN
LVHW010605100826
845148LV00014B/2859